D0734665

MARTIN LUTHER KING, JR.
AND THE FREEDOM MOVEMENT

MARTIN LUTHER KING, JR. AND THE FREEDOM MOVEMENT

LILLIE PATTERSON

☑
Facts On File
New York • Oxford

Martin Luther King, Jr. and the Freedom Movement

Facts On File,® Inc.
460 Park Avenue South
New York, New York 10016

Library of Congress Cataloging-in-Publication Data

Patterson, Lillie.
    Martin Luther King, Jr. and the freedom movement / Lillie
Patterson.
        p. cm. — (Makers of America)
    Bibliography: p.
    Includes index.
    Summary: A biography of the Baptist minister, focusing on his
leadership role in the civil rights movement.
    ISBN 0-8160-1605-4
    1. King, Martin Luther, Jr., 1929-1968. 2. Afro-Americans—
Biography. 3. Baptists—United States—Clergy—Biography.
4. Segregation in transportation—Alabama—Birmingham—History—20th
century. 5. Afro-Americans—Civil rights. 6. Birmingham (Ala.)—
Race relations. [1. King, Martin Luther, Jr., 1929-1968.
2. Civil rights workers. 3. Clergy. 4. Afro-Americans—Biography.]
I. Title. II. Series: Makers of America (Facts On File, Inc.)
323.4'092'4—dc19
[B]
[92]
                                                                    88-26051

Text Design by Debbie Glasserman
Jacket Design by Duane Stapp
Composition by Facts On File Inc/Maxwell Photographics
Printed in the United States of America

10 9 8 7 6 5 4 3 2 1

This book honors the young people of all races who caught Dr. King's vision of a more humane nation and helped him to dramatize this dream so others could understand.

CONTENTS

PREFACE

After an assassin's bullet ended his life prematurely in 1968, Martin Luther King, Jr. was carried to his grave in the way he had planned, on a wagon drawn by a mule. His own fate, he believed, was not important. The power to save the world lay with millions of people and their commitment to nonviolent struggle.

Nearly twenty years later, even though a national holiday had been established in his honor, it seemed as though Martin King's message had been forgotten. American leaders, it is true, now applauded the dream of equal rights for all, which King had proclaimed from the steps of the Lincoln Memorial on August 28, 1963, yet few drew attention to the fact that for Martin King the battle for civil rights was only one front, even if an important one, in a worldwide struggle against what he called "the terrible midnight of our age."

Martin Luther King did not believe that all that blacks needed was "a fair share of the nation's pie." The pie itself, he said, was poisoned. Americans, he warned, despite their vast technological power, faced a mortal threat. The United States failed to confront the unending war, the worldwide arms race, the racism, and the poverty that were engulfing humankind. "Your moral progress lags behind your scientific progress," he said. "Your mentality outdistances your morality; your civilization outshines your culture."

People in our society, he went on, have found it easy to accept the suffering that is daily endured by those of other faiths, other races, and other nationalities. "We fail to see them as fellow human beings, made from the same basic stuff as we." But this common humanity, he believed, is a basic fact of life. Love is a unifying principle, lying at the center of the cosmos.

Freedom for all Americans, not merely freedom for black people, was a target of the freedom struggle that he led. "We need a vision," he said, "to see in this generation's ordeals the opportunity to transfigure both ourselves and American society. Our present suffering and our nonviolent struggle to be free may well offer to Western civilization the kind of spiritual dynamic so desperately needed for survival."

Martin King predicted the inevitable decay of any system based on principles "not in harmony with the moral laws of the universe." He preached a revolutionary gospel of nonviolent action not only against racial injustice but against all injustice.

When King was murdered in the spring of 1968, he was groping his way toward an all-embracing movement for human freedom. The Poor People's Campaign, which he launched that year, brought white, black, Hispanic, and Native American people to Washington with a common agenda for economic rights. King, in denouncing American involvement in the Vietnam War, had also gone far beyond the immediate aims of the civil rights movement. His leadership aroused opposition from many who believed that he ought to mind his own business—the business of "winning for black people a piece of the American pie."

Before Martin King died he saw other great struggles sprout from the civil rights movement—struggles for equal rights for women, for lesbians and gays, for peace and disarmament, for the survival of the planet itself menaced by pollution, waste, and greed.

During the years that followed King's death many questioned the value of nonviolent action, even of any action at all. Robert Kennedy's assassination, Watergate, and a virtual end to federal commitment to the struggle against poverty and want all reinforced a mood of cynicism and despair. It almost seemed as though the dream of nonviolent mass action to reshape a troubled world had died with Martin King. Was this the sum total of his legacy, some people asked, just another day off from work?

In actual fact Martin Luther King, Jr.'s memory remains bright in the hearts of the young. In 1988 an opinion poll found that among young people born since his death King ranks number one as a hero.

Today the freedom movement of which he dreamed has become a major political force in the United States. This book tells the story of King's deep and passionate beliefs, which he expressed not only in words but always and above all in actions.

1

THE MONTGOMERY BUS BOYCOTT, 1955–1956

Rosa Parks, a diminutive black woman of forty-three, boarded a crowded city bus in Montgomery, Alabama. It was Thursday, December 1, 1955. Weary from work as a tailor's assistant in a downtown store, she sat in an aisle seat directly behind the section reserved for white riders. This was the "neutral zone."

Soon all the front seats were filled; a white man was standing. The bus driver looked around at four black riders sitting behind the "whites only" sign. "You all better make it light on yourselves and give me those seats," he said.

A man and two women stood up. Rosa Parks stayed put.

Riders watched the scene in tense silence. All knew the city ordinance on bus transportation. Blacks must sit in the back. When all seats in the "whites only" section were taken, black riders in the "neutral zone" must give up their seats and stand. Bus drivers, all of whom were white, had the power to arrest black riders who refused to obey the law.

The driver, James Blake, stopped the bus. "Look woman, I told you I wanted the seat. Are you going to stand up?" There was fury in his voice.

"No," said Parks, the eyes behind her rimless glasses never wavering.

"Well, if you don't stand I am going to have you arrested."

"Go on and have me arrested," said Rosa Parks.

Blake telephoned the police, and soon a patrol car arrived.

"Why didn't you stand up?" asked the officer.

"I did not think that I should have to stand up. After I had paid my fare and occupied a seat, I didn't think I should have to give it up."

Rosa Parks was taken away in the squad car. Black riders in the bus looked at one another and shook their heads. Defiance of the segregation laws had often led to jailing, beating, even death.

A telephone call to E. D. Nixon brought him in haste to the police station. Nixon was local organizer of the Brotherhood of Sleeping Car Porters, the union of black railroad workers. He posted bond for Mrs. Parks' release on bail. Then he began to call together community leaders. The Women's Political Council also went into action.

Rosa Parks is fingerprinted following her arrest. (AP/Wide World)

The following evening, Friday, December 2, these people held a planning meeting at the Dexter Avenue Baptist Church, where Reverend Martin Luther King, Jr. was the minister. The idea of starting a bus boycott had been germinating for months. Rosa Parks had now provided the needed spark: a dramatic incident and a person around whom black citizens could rally. Mrs. Parks was an ideal symbol for the cause. Well-known and highly respected, she had a radiant personality; for ten years she had worked for the National Association for the Advancement of Colored People (NAACP) as Nixon's secretary.

Rev. Martin Luther King, Jr. was happy to join the planners. He had arrived in Montgomery scarcely a year earlier to take up his job as Dexter's new minister. His solid brick church with its high bell tower occupied a prominent spot on a beautiful public square across from the state capitol with its gleaming white dome and stately portico.

Martin King's first months at Dexter throughout 1955 had taught him how fear and petty squabbles kept the black community from joining together for common goals. Would they now unite, he asked himself, to protest against segregation on buses? Dexter's large meeting room was in the basement of the church. Every black community organization was represented at the gathering that Martin King found there. "I knew," he recalled, "that something unusual was about to happen."

The meeting began. After some discussion everybody there endorsed the proposal for a bus boycott. The group then broke up into committees to make the necessary preparations. A transportation committee outlined ways for people to get to their jobs without having to ride the buses. Ministers pooled ideas for taking the news to church members and winning their support. Martin King worked with Jo Ann Robinson, president of the Women's Political Council, to revise a leaflet that she had drafted for distribution the next day, Saturday, December 3. King said that he would do the mimeographing early in the morning.

They all worked until late in the evening; it was nearly twelve o'clock before the group left the church. "The clock on the wall read almost midnight," King said later, "but the clock in our souls revealed that it was daybreak."

Tired but elated, the young minister drove back home to the parsonage to share the news with his wife, Coretta. He had met and married the beautiful, talented music major while they were both students in Boston. Their first months in Montgomery had been filled with happiness. King completed his dissertation and received his doctorate from Boston University in June 1955. Five months later Yolanda Denise, their first child, was born. Her father called her Yoki for short.

During those early months King took an active part in the life of the black community. He became a board member of the local NAACP and a fund-raiser. He gained a reputation as a fine speaker. He also worked with the Alabama Council on Human Relations, one of the few interracial organizations in the state. He was busy at meetings of one kind or another nearly every night of the week.

Martin and Coretta King with baby Yolanda Denise (Yoki) on the steps of Dexter Avenue Baptist Church. (Dan Weiner, courtesy of Sandra Weiner/MAGNUM)

Saturday morning the mimeograph machine at Dexter whirred and clacked as King and his secretary ran off seven thousand leaflets. Two hours later Jo Ann Robinson picked them up; squadrons of women and teenagers passed them around in the black neighborhoods. The message was brief and to the point:

Don't ride the bus to work, to town, to school, or any place Monday, December 5.

Another Negro woman has been arrested and put in jail because she refused to give up her bus seat.

Don't ride the buses . . . . If you work, take a cab, or share a ride, or walk.

Come to a mass meeting, Monday at 7.00 P.M., at the Holt Street Baptist Church for further instruction.

Blacks read the leaflets. They remembered many insulting experiences aboard city buses. During the past year alone four women had been arrested for refusing to give up their seats. The city bus company employed only white drivers, even though 70 percent of all riders were black. These practices were part of a system of discrimination against black people dating back to slavery days. White slave masters believed that they were superior beings. They treated their black slaves like horses or cattle, never as equals.

On Sunday, December 4, black ministers gave out the message at their regular church services. "Don't ride the buses tomorrow!" they urged their congregations.

The local newspaper, the *Montgomery Advertiser,* helped with unexpected publicity. An article in the paper attacked the boycott. "Racism," the *Advertiser* called it.

The article disturbed Martin King. He sat in his den that Sunday afternoon and faced its shelves with their many books dealing with theology, philosophy, Christianity, ethics. Was the boycott unethical?

His answer finally came from Henry David Thoreau, one of his favorite American philosophers. People, Thoreau wrote, should be governed by their conscience; they should refuse to obey unjust laws. Black citizens, King reasoned, were not seeking to destroy the bus company but the practices of the company that supported and enforced an evil system. Black people ought to refuse to support the company, or ride its buses, until the system was changed.

Martin King went to bed. Nagging questions kept him awake. Would years of intimidation cause blacks to shrink from launching a movement of protest? What would happen if violence broke out? What if the boycott fizzled? This might dampen hopes of challenging segregation elsewhere in the South.

Monday, December 5, Martin and Coretta King were up before dawn. From their living room windows they watched for the first bus to come down Jackson Street, a route taken mostly by black passengers. Coretta saw the bus first. "Darling, it's empty! empty!"

A second bus came. The driver sat alone, rows of vacant seats behind him. King drove away to pick up Reverend Ralph Abernathy, pastor of Montgomery's First Baptist Church, and a close friend. Together they cruised the streets, counting less than a dozen black riders on the buses. The boycott seemed close to 100 percent.

All that day black people walked the streets, smiling and waving; others rode mules; and some even fixed up old horse-drawn buggies to get around in. Those in cars or taxis stopped to squeeze in one more passenger. Grade school children waved at the empty buses, cheered, and called out, "No riders today!" The one-day boycott marked a milestone in Montgomery's history.

Martin King drove to the police court for Rosa Parks' trial. Had the judge dismissed the case, or had he fined Mrs. Parks on the usual "disorderly conduct" charge, the matter might have ended. Instead she was convicted of disobeying a state law that required segregation in public transportation. Fred Gray, Mrs. Parks' twenty-five-year-old counsel, announced that she would appeal. She would challenge the con- stitutionality of the Alabama segregation statute.

Boycott leaders, along with King, planning for the mass meeting that was to be held that Monday evening, agreed that a permanent organization ought to be set up to guide the coming struggle. Rev. Abernathy suggested a name: the Montgomery Improvement Association (MIA). A president would be needed, a person of courage, gifted with the eloquence to speak for a united black community. From a corner of the room Rufus Lewis, a businessman, called out: "Mr. Chairman, I would like to nominate Reverend M. L. King."

Martin King accepted the nomination. "Somebody has to do it," he said, "and if you think I can, I will serve." A resolution was drawn up for presention at the evening's rally. The audience would vote to decide whether or not to go on with the boycott.

The evening meeting was held at the Holt Street Baptist Church. When King arrived he found the building crowded, with hundreds of people spilling out onto the streets. A loudspeaker had been set up on the roof to broadcast the program to listeners outside.

Prayers and songs opened the meeting. Rosa Parks was introduced and received a standing ovation. Martin King came forward to speak; there was a hush. He looked young, so vulnerable, with a face indescribably winsome in its appeal. Old women at Dexter, who adored him, often said that their pastor "looks like he ought to still be home with his mama."

King had outlined his speech on paper before he left home that night. But as he looked at the upturned faces of the crowd, he suddenly felt no need for outlines or notes. He spoke, as a preacher should, from the heart.

"We are here," he began, "because we are American citizens, and we are determined to acquire our citizenship to the fullest of its meaning. . . . We are here this evening to say to those who have mistreated us so long, that we are tired—tired of being segregated and humiliated; tired of being kicked about by the brutal feet of oppression."

The speaker moved from words of indignation to those of peace. "If you will protest courageously, and yet with

Christian love, . . . the historians will have to pause and say, 'There lived a great people—a black people—who injected new meaning and dignity into the veins of civilization.'" With one sixteen-minute speech King turned a one-day boycott into an ongoing protest movement.

Rev. Abernathy rose to his feet and presented the demands that the bus company must meet before blacks would once more use the buses:

> Polite treatment from bus drivers; first-come, first-served seating, with blacks seating from the rear forward, whites from the front; hiring of black bus drivers for routes in neighborhoods with mostly black riders.

The call for voting rang through the church. "All in favor, let it be known by standing." The crowd stood up; the people listening outside cheered. "They were on fire," wrote a reporter, "for freedom."

Montgomery, first capital of the Confederacy, had become the starting place of a social revolution. The movement, as King wrote later, "would gain national recognition, . . . would ring in the ears of people of every nation; . . . would astound the oppressor, and bring hope to the oppressed."

The boycott went on. One day an old woman trudged along the street, weary, straight-shouldered, proud. A passing driver stopped his car and called out "Jump in, grandmother, you don't need to walk." She smiled and waved him on. "I'm not walking for myself," she said: "I'm walking for my children and my grandchildren."

Transportation was the biggest problem. Blacks made up 40 percent of Montgomery's population of 124,000. Nearly one-half of the men and two-thirds of the women worked as laborers or domestics, usually miles from their homes. To get to work they depended largely upon the buses. The MIA solved the problem with a combination of share-a-ride cooperation and cheap taxi service, provided by black-owned taxicab companies. Many people preferred to walk as a symbol of freedom.

City officials soon put an end to the cheap cab rides. They threatened the taxi companies with an old city ordinance that set a minimum taxi fare that must be charged. The MIA's response to this was a car-pooling plan, with a communications network to link up riders and drivers. Within three days, three hundred drivers had come forward to operate this service.

The MIA Transportation Committee dotted a city map with points for forty-eight dispatch and forty-two pickup stations. Every morning, churches looked like bus stations, with waiting riders using them as shelters from the cold. Business and professional people played their part. One pharmacist could be seen filling prescriptions with his hands while giving dispatch information into the phone. College students, teachers, housewives, all drove whenever their schedules permitted. Some workers started out early, carried others to their jobs, then went on to their own daily duties. Afternoons, they brought their riders back.

The new spirit toppled barriers that had kept black people apart before. Rich and poor, young and old, college professors and nonliterates, all faced hardships in order to win equality.

January 1956: the boycott went on. King was alerted to the dangers of violence from racist groups like the Ku Klux Klan. Week after week at the mass meetings he warned the people against the use of violence. "We must meet the forces of hate with the power of love," he reminded them. The MIA's slogan became "Justice without violence."

Hate mail and hateful telephone calls descended daily upon Martin and Coretta King's home. "Get out of town or else!" the voices threatened: "Did you know you have a short time to live?"

The boycott went on. At first Mayor Gayle and Montgomery city officials regarded it merely as a nuisance that would quickly fizzle. Soon they understood the new mood of iron determination that was in the black community. The police now started to get tough. Pool drivers were arrested upon the slightest pretext; rumors were spread that drivers' permits and car insurance might be canceled. King himself was arrested one day while driving passengers. The police let him go when hundreds of furious people came storming down to the station house.

One night toward the end of January 1956, King lay in bed, trying to relax after a long hard day. The telephone rang; late night calls had become routine since the boycott began. This one was different. "Listen, nigger," a voice snarled, "we've taken all we want from you. Before next week you'll be sorry you ever came to Montgomery."

All of a sudden the young minister realized his utter exhaustion. The weeks of superhuman schedules had taken their toll. Could he go on? Tiptoeing out to the kitchen he made a cup of coffee and tried to think it through. At any moment a bomb could snuff out the lives of Coretta and Yoki. At any moment the threats to kill him could become real.

Martin King was afraid.

At the end of his own powers, he put his head in his hands and prayed to God for help. "Almost at once," he remembered later, "my fears began to go, I was ready to face anything. . . ." At age 27 Martin King overcame the fear of death and danger. So long as he remained a leader in the struggle for human rights, death would remain but a shadow's length away. He decided to make every single moment of his life count, to face each single test with all his faith.

The first test came soon.

On January 30 King addressed a gathering at Abernathy's church. As he was speaking somebody beckoned Abernathy aside and whispered a message.

King stopped speaking. "What's wrong?" he asked.

"Your house has been bombed," Abernathy replied.

"Are Coretta and the baby all right?"

"We are checking on that now. We think so."

Before leaving for home King took a moment to let the congregation know what had happened. He was visibly shaken. "Let us keep moving," he told them, "with the faith that what we are doing is right, . . . that God is with us in the struggle."

Black people were milling around the parsonage as he approached it; policemen were trying to hold the crowd back. The bomb had blown apart pillars supporting the front porch. Shattered windows had showered glass over the living room floor. Mayor Gayle was there, his face pale, offering regrets. Squeezing by, King went in to find his wife and child. Both were safe.

Outside the crowd grew bigger; there was anger, tension. Many people had picked up the first weapon they could find as they rushed to the scene of the explosion. The slightest incident—an angry word, a blow—could set off a race riot.

Martin King went out onto the porch. He held up his hand; his gesture quieted the crowd. He reminded the people of the principles that had guided them thus far. "We must meet hate with love," he told them. "Remember, if I am stopped the movement will not stop, because God is with this movement. Go home with this glowing faith and this radiant reassurance."

It was a moonlit night; tears glistened on the upturned faces. One by one the people turned and left. Their words floated back to Martin King's ears like a benediction. "We're with you all the way, Reverend." "Amen, amen."

The next day newspapers throughout America carried pictures of the young minister teaching love and forgiveness from his bombed porch. The photos elicited a wave of sympathy. Every mail brought letters of encouragement.

The boycott went on; the economic squeeze tightened. Downtown stores suffered from the loss of their black customers. The bus company faced bankruptcy. But the city commissioners would not budge. Nor would the black people; they were determined to win, no matter how long it took.

The battle continued not only in the streets but in the courts. City lawyers saw to it that Rosa Parks' appeal was not scheduled for argument; and this blocked the MIA plan to take her case up on appeal. In February the MIA got around this roadblock with a new case. Attorney Fred Gray filed suit in U.S. District Court on behalf of four black women who charged that Alabama's transportation law violated their rights under the U.S. Constitution, specifically the Fourteenth Amendment.

The Fourteenth Amendment had been passed after the end of the Civil War, in 1868. Its purpose was to guarantee to all black people the rights of citizenship and freedom denied to them during two centuries of slavery. The people in Montgomery's streets were battling to breathe new life into a part of the Constitution that, as far as blacks were concerned, had been dead and buried for nearly a century.

City leaders struck back. In February 1956 an all-white grand jury indicted more than one hundred black leaders, at least twenty-four of whom were ministers. They were charged with deliberate violation of state and city laws. E. D. Nixon led the way to the police station to be booked and fingerprinted. "Are you looking for me?" he shouted. "Well, here I am." Close behind was Rosa Parks. Martin King came in, accompanied by Ralph Abernathy. The nation saw him on TV wearing his identification number, 7089, around his neck.

More and more people in other communities now became involved. Support groups organized to raise funds. In New York City an interracial group formed an organization called "In Friendship." "In Friendship," along with financial help, sent observers to Montgomery who wrote articles and offered help with legal and other problems.

Bayard Rustin was one such observer who came to Montgomery to help. One day in February Coretta answered the door. There stood a tall, distinguished-looking black man who radiated energy. She remembered him as a speaker who had visited Antioch College when she was a student there. Rustin, a long-time civil rights activist, was a singer with a magnificent tenor voice. He was also a brilliant organizer who expressed his thoughts in precise, clipped tones. He helped King to shape the last, critical phase of the bus boycott. It was the first of many services that Rustin would contribute to Martin Luther King and his movement.

March 19: supporters packed the Montgomery courthouse for the trial of the black leaders. Hundreds more stood outside. Some wore white crosses with the words: "Father forgive them."

The first to come to trial was Martin Luther King, Jr. Fred Gray and a team of NAACP lawyers used the courtroom to turn the tables and to indict the city for its abuse of black people. Black citizens who had been made victims of violence or abuse while riding the buses were called upon to tell their stories. Mrs. Stella Brooks told how her husband asked for the refund of his fare when the bus was too crowded. The driver put him off and summoned the police, who shot Mr. Brooks to death.

Mrs. Martha Walker told how a bus driver closed the door upon her blind husband, and then started the bus, dragging Mr. Walker by the legs for several blocks. One lady was called "an ugly ape," another "a black cow." A rider who paid her fare up front on a crowded bus was forced to get off and come back in by the rear door. Before she could get back in, the driver pulled away.

On and on, the litany of atrocities unfolded. Surely, the lawyers argued, there were grounds for the boycott. Not so, ruled the judge. He sentenced Martin King to pay a fine and court costs, or spend three-hundred eighty-six days at hard labor on the county farm. The sentence was immediately appealed to a higher court. This test case held up the trial of the other defendants indefinitely.

As King came out of the courthouse supporters lined the sidewalks to greet him. "The protest goes on!" he said. "King is king!" they answered.

Such scenes made compelling human interest stories. Journalists recognized King's value as a news maker. He was handsome, faultlessly dressed, articulate. In interviews he gave elegantly phrased and highly quotable replies to questions. Years of academic training gave him confidence unusual in a young man at the beginning of his career.

Winter turned to spring: the protest went on. In May a panel of judges began hearings on the lawsuit brought by the four women to challenge segregation on Montgomery's buses. The suit had been brought in federal district court, where there was a better chance of getting a fair hearing.

The federal district court ruled that Montgomery's segregated bus system was in violation of the Fourteenth Amendment to the Constitution, and therefore illegal. The city appealed. The case went all the way up to the Supreme Court of the United States for a final decision.

Autumn arrived, bringing to Alabama its paisley-patterned splendor. City leaders decided to strike a final blow against the car pool. A new lawsuit charged MIA with running a transportation system and operating without license fee or franchise. If the city won its case, MIA would be forced to abandon the car pools—the riders' main substitute for the buses.

King shrank from telling his people the news of this formidable attack. At a mass meeting the night before the court hearing, he told them that car pooling might end. Never despair, he added: "This may well be the darkest hour before the dawn."

Next day, November 13, the court hearing began. King sat at a front table as chief defendant. At about noon there was a sudden flurry of activity in the room: A messenger whispered to the judge; the judge whispered to city attorneys. Moments later a reporter passed King a wire services report. He read the words upon it, and, as he wrote later, "my heart began to throb with inexpressible joy."

"The United States Supreme Court," said the report, "today affirmed a decision of a special three-judge U.S. District Court in declaring Alabama's state and local laws supporting segregation on buses unconstitutional."

The Montgomery Improvement Association, led by Martin King, had won its year-long struggle.

The following night the people celebrated their victory in mass meetings held in two churches, with speakers traveling from one to the other. Over 8,000 joined in. Reverend Graetz, a young white minister who had supported the boycott from the beginning, read the scripture. It was from St. Paul's letter to the Corinthians. "When I was a child," he read, "I spake as a child, I understood as a child, I thought as a child. But when I became a man, I put away childish things." People were weeping openly as he finished.

☆ ☆ ☆

Late in December Dr. Martin Luther King, Jr. waited once again before dawn for the first bus to come down Jackson Street; with him were Glenn Smiley, a white minister, Rosa Parks, Ralph Abernathy, and E. D. Nixon. Many ministers had agreed to ride the buses on the first day that the people began to patronize them again and encourage the riders to stay calm and friendly.

A bus arrived. The front door opened. King stepped aboard and paid his fare. The driver smiled a welcome. "We are glad to have you with us this morning," he said.

All over Montgomery black riders boarded buses and sat wherever they pleased.

2

STRONG SOUTHERN ROOTS,
1929–1954

> Who can best lead the South out of
> the social and economic quagmire?
> Her native sons. Those who were
> born and bred in her rich and fertile
> soil; those who love her because they
> were nurtured by her.
>
> MLK

W ho is this Martin Luther King, Jr.?
People around the world wanted to know more about the boycott leader who had orbited so suddenly to fame. News articles and biographical sketches began to publicize his family roots.

His life began in Atlanta, a city that mirrored the charm of a Deep South town, with flowering dogwoods and magnificent magnolias. By the twentieth century the charm blended with tremendous industrial growth. Atlanta flourished as the chief financial, commercial, and transportation hub of the southeastern United States. The city resembled a Northern metropolitan center but kept its natural beauty and its fame as "a city of trees."

Atlanta's black citizens loved the city. Many who came to study or teach in the six colleges for black students settled there to live. In 1930, blacks made up roughly 90,000 of the population, as compared to around 166,000 whites.

A popular saying among both races ran, "Even if you are going to heaven, you've got to come through Atlanta." If you were black you came through legendary "Sweet Auburn," an avenue on the edge of downtown. On Auburn Avenue flourished some of the biggest black-owned businesses in the world—banks, corporations, drugstores, insurance companies . . . Uphill on Auburn stood an attractive community of homes of middle-class black families. At 501 Auburn, in a twelve-room, two-story gray and white Victorian frame house lived Martin Luther King, Sr., a Baptist minister, and his wife, Alberta, a teacher. On the morning of January 15, 1929, their first son, Martin Luther King, Jr., was born.

The birthplace of Dr. Martin Luther King, Jr. on Auburn Avenue in Atlanta. (AP/Wide World)

The boy was born into a family whose name in Atlanta was legendary. His mother's father, Adam Daniel Williams, was born the year the Emancipation Proclamation ended slavery, and throughout his life worked to end injustices against Atlanta's black citizens. Reverend Williams built the Ebenezer Baptist Church from a struggling group of worshipers into one of Atlanta's largest black congregations. When the NAACP was founded in 1909, he helped to organize the Atlanta Chapter and became its president. The organization led a protest that forced the building of the city's first high school for black students. When a local newspaper, the *Georgian,* called NAACP members "dirty and ignorant," Williams organized a boycott and six thousand black subscribers canceled in one day. The newspaper went bankrupt.

The father of the boy born that cold January 15 was also a fearless fighter for equal rights. He was born Michael Luther King in Stockbridge, Georgia in 1899. He later legally changed his name to Martin Luther King. Close friends called him Mike. His father was a cotton farm sharecropper, an occupation forced upon countless poor black families in the Deep South after slavery. White landowners furnished farms and seeds for penniless, landless, black families. Profits were supposedly divided equally between sharecroppers and landowners. Since landowners kept the records, tenants, often poorly educated, could be exploited easily and usually reaped little or no profit and stayed in debt.

One day Mike King, a sturdy barrel-chested teenager, slung his only pair of shoes over his shoulder and walked the twenty miles to Atlanta, determined to have a different kind of life. He worked at an assortment of jobs and attended night school. In his autobiography, *Daddy King,* he recalls the day that changed his life. "I had first seen Alberta Williams on Auburn Avenue. . . . I was a student at Bryant Preparatory School and she was a boarding student at Spelman." The daughter of Reverend Adam Daniel Williams had fractured her ankle and was walking on crutches near her home. Mike, the country boy, fell in love at first sight of the poised, fashionably dressed student, who was also a talented musician. "When I told my buddies that I'd fallen in love with Miss Williams and planned to marry her," he wrote, "they thought I'd lost my mind or religion, or both!"

One friend scoffed and teased. "That's the worst-looking story I've heard all year—you marrying Alberta Williams. Go on away from here."

So Mike King began to study harder, carrying books wherever he worked. He soon began to preach in small churches that were being organized. Each time he passed along 501 Auburn Avenue he hoped for a glimpse of Alberta. One day she smiled in her shy way, and that was the beginning of their courtship. "My little bunch of goodness," he called her, later shortening the endearment to "Bunch." She finished her studies at Spelman and at Hampton Institute in Virginia. Mike King continued his education at Morehouse, the private college for black males. The two were married in Ebenezer in 1926, with three ministers officiating.

Ebenezer Baptist Church, Atlanta, where Martin Luther King, Jr., his father, and his maternal grandfather served as ministers. (AP/Wide World)

The newlyweds moved into the separate apartment on the second floor of 501 Auburn. In time Mike King, Sr. became assistant pastor to his father-in-law. When Reverend Williams died suddenly in 1931, Ebenezer appointed Reverend King as pastor.

It was to this intriguing family tree that the name of Martin Luther King, Jr. was added in 1929. Church members nicknamed him "M. L.", or "Little Mike," to distinguish him from his father. With sister Willie Christine, a year older, and brother Alfred Daniel, a year younger, he enjoyed a happy, normal childhood.

Life for the King family revolved around Ebenezer, only a short walk from their home. From early childhood M. L. was fascinated by words and music. As he listened to his father's rousing sermons he learned the power of words to sway emotions when set in rhythmic patterns and spoken in spellbinding eloquence. He sensed the power of music as he listened to the soul-stirring singing, while his mother played the organ. Music brought emotional release to people weighed down with daily problems of trying to exist in a world that treated them as lesser beings. By the time he was six, M. L. was singing solos, with Mother Dear, as he called Alberta King, accompanying him at the organ.

As M. L. grew older, he felt the impact of signs and laws that kept black and white people segregated. Black children growing up in the South learned two words as early as they learned ABC's: *colored* and *white*. Bold signs restricted their worlds and conditioned their minds—WHITES ONLY—COLORED SCHOOL—NIGGERS AND DOGS KEEP OUT!

One day six-year-old M. L. ran to his mother. Two young white friends told him their mother did not want them to continue playing with a black boy.

"Why?" M. L. questioned his mother.

Gently, Alberta King explained the whys of American slavery and its aftermath of a segregated society. White owners saw slaves as "property" to be bought or sold, not as equals. When slavery ended, amendments were added to the

Constitution to protect the rights of blacks. But, Southern states passed "Jim Crow" laws to make sure that black and white races remained segregated as in the time of slavery. The term "Jim Crow" came from a minstrel show character. Through the years, Jim Crow laws reinforced the idea of black inferiority, white supremacy. But as generations of blacks became better educated, these insulting laws were harder to accept.

Alberta King did what other black mothers learned to do. She soothed her son's hurt with the reassurance, "You are as good as anyone, and don't you ever forget it."

Daddy King was more of a fighter. From early boyhood M. L. watched his proud, fearless father protest injustices against black citizens. One day he was in the car when a traffic cop stopped Daddy King. "All right, boy," the cop ordered, "pull over and let me see your license."

Neither blaring sirens nor menacing stares of a white officer intimidated the minister. He looked the officer straight in the eye. "That's the boy there," he said, pointing to M. L. "I'm a man. I'm Reverend King." The boldness confused the cop into politeness. "O.K. You're a man. Now let me see your license."

On another day, M. L. and his father shopped for shoes. They took seats in the front of a store. A clerk asked them to move to back seats, where black customers sat in Southern shoe stores. The fury on Daddy King's face matched his scorching reply. "We'll buy shoes sitting here, or we won't buy any shoes at all." He continued sitting to show disdain, then, taking M. L.'s hands, he gave the clerk a withering look and strode from the store as majestically as though he had received service reserved for royalty.

There were other incidents that demonstrated Daddy King's courage. He rallied more than a thousand black citizens at Ebenezer for a 1935 march on City Hall as part of a voting rights drive. The next year he opened his home as a meeting place for black teachers protesting the Southern practice of paying black teachers less than their white colleagues. Daddy King kept crusading, despite threats and hate letters from segregationists. Some letters came with drawings of a coffin—with the minister pictured as a corpse inside. When church members had problems—police, bank, hospital, or whatever—they came to Daddy King. He would barge into an establishment and call out, "Where's the top man's office?" Black and white alike knew him as a "man who don't take no stuff." He often got results, too.

Despite segregation, M. L.'s parents made sure that his childhood was secure and happy. Grandmother Jennie Celeste Williams loved her three grandchildren dearly, and helped with their upbringing. M. L. was her favorite. He called her "Mama," and she cooked his favorite dishes and read stories from the Bible to him. He delighted in reciting long biblical passages from memory.

Tragedy touched his life the year he was twelve. One day when he was supposed to be in his room studying, he sneaked away to watch a parade. While he was gone, Grandmother Jennie suffered a heart attack while speaking on a Woman's Day Program and died on the way to the hospital. The sensitive boy believed that his misbehavior had caused her death. Daddy King finally convinced him that Grandmother Jennie's death was not his fault, reminding him, "God had His own plan and His own way. . . ."

In 1941, Daddy King moved his family into a large house he dreamed of owning since he was a penniless youth. Soon afterward a new and larger Ebenezer was built. Meanwhile, young Mike moved toward his teen years. After attending the Daniel T. Howard Elementary School he enrolled in the Atlanta University Laboratory School for seventh and eighth grades. When this school closed, he transferred to the public Booker T. Washington High School, built because of his grandfather's crusading. He continued his interest in music and learned to play the piano and violin.

M. L.'s wide reading helped him to become a champion debater. An eleventh grader, he traveled to a South Georgia town with his speech teacher, Mrs. Sarah Bradley, to compete against other students. He spoke on "The Negro and the Constitution," and captured one of the prizes. In a jubilant mood teacher and prizewinner took a crowded bus to return home. At a stop along the way white passengers came aboard. The white driver ordered King and his teacher to give up their seats. Years later he still talked about that incident: "I intended to stay right in that seat, but Mrs. Bradley finally urged me up, saying we had to obey the law. And so we stood up in the aisle for the ninety miles to Atlanta. That night will never leave my memory. It was the angriest I have ever been in my life."

M. L. skipped two grades, ninth and twelfth, and entered Morehouse College when he was only fifteen. The college had become known for graduating men who became leaders. The campus, dotted with magnificent trees and ivy-covered buildings, presented an atmosphere of beauty and dignity. To be a "Morehouse Man" carried a tradition of responsibility, success, and service.

From his freshman year, young King took an active part in student life. He sang in the glee club and, despite his small size, played on the football team. He helped to develop the college Youth Chapter of the NAACP. His work with the Intercollegiate Council, composed of black and white students from neighboring colleges, helped to mellow his thinking about black-white relationships. "The wholesome relation we had with this group," he remembered, "convinced me that we have many white persons as allies, particularly among the younger generation."

College friends called him Mike more than M. L. Mike balanced his serious studies with the fun of college life. Close friends nicknamed him "Tweed" because of his classy style of dressing. His popularity with girls delighted his younger brother, A. D. "He had his share of girlfriends and I decided I couldn't keep up with him," A. D. recalled, "He was crazy about dances and was just about the best jitterbug in town. . . ."

Inspiration from several brilliant professors influenced Mike's intellectual development and career choice. Professor Gladstone Lewis Chandler, a pipe-smoking, articulate Harvard graduate, encouraged students in his English classes to learn and use new, unusual words. Under his guidance, Mike learned to write clear, concise speeches. Professor George D. Kelsey, the scholarly director of religious studies, taught students the responsibilities of preachers. Ministers, he believed, must be philosophers and search for ways to solve social problems.

Morehouse president Dr. Benjamin Mays, a minister and a close friend to Daddy King, had perhaps the greatest influence on Mike's choice of a career. Each Tuesday morning the suave, eloquent minister addressed the four-hundred-odd students during required chapel services. His silvery hair, his Phi Beta Kappa key, symbol of high scholastic rank, presented a study in elegance. In his powerful style of delivery, Rev. Dr. Mays urged students to follow careers that involved scholarship and service. "There are some faces one notices," Dr. Mays said later. He noticed Mike King's intense listening and note taking. Many times Mike would stop by the president's office to discuss points he had made in a speech.

The summer of 1947 M. L. King joined schoolmates and worked on tobacco farms in Connecticut. Until then he planned to become a doctor or lawyer and fight segregation through the courts. That summer he wrote his mother of new plans: "You know, daddy won't believe me, but I'm going to preach." Alberta King was overjoyed. So was Daddy King, but he questioned his son. "Are you serious about this?"

Mike's answer was firm. "Yes sir, I'm going to preach."

Rev. King arranged for his son to preach a trial sermon at Ebenezer. On the day chosen, a large crowd filled the church to hear their pastor's son preach his first sermon. Wearing a white surplice, young King spoke that Sunday about human suffering. Daddy King listened to the sincerity and power of his son's delivery and decided, "Well, there was nothing to do but go on and license him." Later he told how he went home and thanked the Lord for having given him such a son. Some Ebenezer members who heard young King went away saying, "The Lord has laid his hands on him." In February 1948, Martin Luther King, Jr. was ordained at Ebenezer in the religious ceremony that admitted him to the Christian ministry. He became his father's assistant at Ebenezer, continuing the family tradition into the third generation.

M. L. graduated from Morehouse at age nineteen and applied to enter Crozer Theological Seminary, a private nondenominational college rated one of the best seminaries in America. On his application blank he wrote that his background had placed upon him "a sense of responsibility which I could not escape." That fall he arrived at the tree-shaded Crozer campus, located in Chester, Pennsylvania. The student body numbered around one hundred. Twelve students were women; six were black. For the first time Martin King attended an integrated school. With a fighting spirit learned from his father, he made up his mind to prove that black students could be as scholarly as those of other races. He earned an A in every course he took. As always, the serious side of Mike King's personality was balanced by his fun-loving, outgoing personality and love of good times. Girls in the area around Crozer vied for his attention.

Crozer's black students found a welcome in the home of Reverend J. Pious Barbour, one of Daddy King's close friends, who pastored a large church. After a feast of Mrs. Barbour's delicious cooking, the minister gave lessons on preaching and encouraged each student to practice different preaching styles. Style, he taught, was as important as content. King developed "the poetic, literary style," Reverend Barbour's daughter remembered. He learned to use cadence and rhythm to create an emotional bond with his audience.

Young Reverend King had found his style, but he continued to search for his ministerial philosophy. Like many college students during the years following World War II, he pondered ways to create harmony among nations and races. "Not until I entered Crozer," he said, "did I begin a serious intellectual quest for a method to eliminate social evil." Two speakers, different in race and speaking style, steered his thinking.

Abraham Johannes Muste, affectionately called "A. J.," the well-known pacifist, came to lecture at Crozer. Trained as a

Presbyterian minister, Muste was executive secretary of the Fellowship of Reconciliation (FOR), an organization active in fostering peace and civil rights. King listened to the tall, white-haired pacifist lecture about peaceful activism in his gentle manner, and took a firmer step toward shaping his own philosophy. "I wasn't a pacifist then," King recalled, "but the power of A. J.'s sincerity and his hardheaded ability to defend his position stayed with me through the years."

A. J. Muste was known as "The American Gandhi." One Sunday Mike King went to nearby Philadelphia to hear Dr. Mordecai Wyatt Johnson lecture at Fellowship House about the real Gandhi. A Morehouse graduate, and the first black president of Howard University in Washington, D.C., the handsome, distinguished-looking minister kept the audience hypnotized by his eloquent description of his trip to India as a member of the World Pacifist Conference. The meeting had been delayed when Mahatma Gandhi, who would have been a participant, was assassinated on January 13, 1948. Mordecai Johnson highlighted Gandhi's long nonviolent campaign against British domination that brought freedom to India. Gandhi won by rallying the masses of poor people and teaching them to refuse to cooperate with unjust practices.

King took from the lectures by Muste and Johnson concepts about organizing the masses of downtrodden black Americans. He immediately went out and bought books about Gandhi. "As I read," he remembered, "I became deeply fascinated by his campaigns on nonviolent resistance."

In June 1951, Martin Luther King, Jr. graduated as valedictorian with an A average. He won the Pearl Plafker Award for his outstanding scholarship and the Lewis Crozer Fellowship, which awarded him $1,200 for graduate studies at the school of his choice. King chose Boston University. That fall he drove his new green Chevrolet, a graduation present from his family, to Boston and began studies toward a Ph.D. in systematic theology at Boston University's School of Theology.

He shared an apartment with Philip Lenud, a Morehouse friend studying for his doctorate at Tufts University. Several other Atlanta students had come to Boston for advanced studies. A popular eating place for them was the Western Lunch Box, specializing in Southern cooking. One winter day in 1952, King lunched there with Mrs. Mary Powell, a long-time friend who was studying music. "Mary," he said wistfully, "I wish I knew a few girls from down home I could go out with."

Mary Powell turned matchmaker. She mentioned names of two girls. He already knew one. Mary then ticked off a description of the second girl: intelligent—lovely—shapely—born in Marion, Alabama—a graduate of Antioch College, studying voice at the New England Conservatory of Music. "She's really charming," Mary Powell insisted. "Her name is Coretta Scott."

"She sounds great," King said, obviously interested.

"I'll ask her if its all right for me to give you her phone number," Mary Powell promised.

King flashed his boyish grin. "While you're at it, put in a good word for me, will you?"

The day he telephoned Coretta Scott, he introduced himself with authority. "This is Martin Luther King." By the time the conversation ended, he had charmed the music student into a luncheon date. The next day in a cold drizzle, he drove to the conservatory to meet her. When Coretta Scott stepped into the car the two students made a quick study of each other. The scarf around her head and the black coat buttoned high against the January chill enhanced her overall wholesome loveliness. She, in turn, made a snap judgment: "How short he seems. How unimpressive he looks." She had pictured a tall man to match the powerful, resonant voice.

Over lunch in a cafeteria, Coretta Scott soon forgot about size. She studied the engaging smile, the almond-shaped eyes, the gentlemanly gestures. "He radiated charm," she wrote later. "When he talked he grew in stature. . . . I knew immediately he was very special."

While they ate, King scrutinized Coretta. The light blue suit complimented the clear, light bronze skin and the sheen of her naturally wavy hair, worn with heavy bangs. More important, he was impressed by her ability to match wits on any topic he brought up. "Oh, you can *think*, too!" he teased. When he drove her home, the student from Atlanta had another surprise for the student from Alabama. "You're everything I'm looking for in a wife," he said quietly. He told her what "everything" was: character, intelligence, personality and beauty. "And you have them all. I want to see you again. When can I?"

Soon—as it turned out. Over the spring and summer the couple attended concerts, skated in the park, danced at parties, and held long discussions. King learned about Coretta's family and her early life. She was born in 1927 in Perry County, Alabama, the second of three children. Her parents, Bernice and Obadiah Scott, struggled to own a large farm and build a store. Her proud, independent parents sent Coretta and her older sister, Edythe, to the Lincoln School, founded by missionaries in the town of Marion, Alabama. Lincoln's interracial staff helped the two girls develop their talents and win college scholarships. Olive Williams, a black music teacher, took a special interest in Coretta, and helped her improve her beautiful singing voice. A scholarship under a work-study program allowed her to attend Antioch College in Yellow Springs, Ohio. After graduating from Antioch, Coretta came to Boston in 1951 to study on another scholarship. She had her heart set on becoming a concert singer.

Daddy and Mother King came to Boston and met their son's new friend. "I knew she was a woman of substance," Daddy King said after he talked to Coretta.

"She is the most important person to come into my life, Dad," his son told him.

Daddy King had deep concerns, however, and he talked them over with his son. At one point he suddenly slammed his big hand down on a table and shouted, "You all are courting too hard. What's this doing to your studies?"

King, Jr. never argued with his strong-willed father. That day he answered quietly and with finality, "I'm going on to get my doctorate, and then I'm going to marry Coretta."

King, Sr. wrote later about that moment. "The young man was so much in love, stars were glittering in his eyes." So Daddy King whammed his hand on the table one more time and said, "Now you two had better get married."

Mike King and Coretta Scott had already talked seriously about marriage. For her, it came to a classic struggle between love and ambition. She had worked and sacrificed and graduated from Antioch and come to the New England Conservatory. Her dream of singing on a concert stage seemed within reach. Could she give this up? ". . . it took me a long time to make up my mind," she recalled in her autobiography.

She made her choice, deciding, "He was such a very good man." She added, "But he was also so alive and funny, and so much fun to be with."

On June 18, 1953, Coretta Scott and Martin Luther King, Jr. were married on the spacious lawn of her parents' home in Marion, Alabama. Daddy King, proud and happy, performed the ceremonies. A. D. was best man.

The newlyweds returned to Boston and set up housekeeping in a four-room rented apartment in an old house. The groom continued working toward his doctorate. The bride shifted her studies to music education, with a major in voice.

By early 1954 King had completed his course requirements and needed only to finish writing his dissertation. Coretta would graduate in June. King began searching for a full-time position. He received several tempting offers from colleges, businesses, and large churches, North and South. He preferred the South. The Jim Crow signs were still there. Changes had come where they could not be seen—in the heart and spirit of black people. These became more evident after the landmark U.S. Supreme Court decision that year.

For years the NAACP had been fighting in the courts against the 1896 *Plessy v. Ferguson* decision that ruled "separate but equal" facilities for blacks legal. In the 1950s NAACP attorneys, headed by Thurgood Marshall, challenged the decision again through a class action suit under the name of one of the school desegregation cases. The suit was filed by Oliver Brown of Topeka, Kansas on behalf of his seven-year-old daughter, Linda. On May 17, 1954, Chief Justice Earl Warren announced the opinion in the *Brown et al v. Board of Education of Topeka* case. "We come then," Chief Justice Warren read, "to the question presented: Does segregation of children in public schools solely on the basis of race . . . deprive the children of the minority group of equal education opportunities? We believe that it does. . . ." He concluded, "Separate educational facilities are inherently unequal." The time seemed right for King to return to the South.

A letter from officers of the Dexter Avenue Baptist church in Montgomery, Alabama intrigued King. They needed a pastor and invited him to come and preach. Since King planned to spend Christmas in Atlanta, he promised to drive to Montgomery afterward. On a Saturday afternoon in January 1954, he saw the city of Montgomery and Dexter.

On Sunday morning his sermon was titled "The Three Dimensions of a Complete Life," based upon the Book of Revelation. He preached about love—love of self, love of neighbor, love of God. Later, church officials invited him to come to Dexter as pastor. "I'll give it my most prayerful and serious consideration," King promised.

The considerations included Coretta's opinion. She liked the idea of living close to her parents. On the other hand, there was the segregated existence, the racism. The couple debated their future. Where should they go? North or South? College or church? The North offered more opportunities for cultural enrichment, for personal growth. Still, Martin King's roots drew him to the South. Coretta supported her husband's decision. The couple moved to Montgomery. Coretta recalled her sense of destiny: "Martin and I and the people of the southern city were like actors in a play, the end of which we had not yet read."

King wrote, "We had the feeling that something remarkable was unfolding in the South, and we wanted to be on hand to witness it."

3

SCLC, THE PRAYER PILGRIMAGE, AND LITTLE ROCK, 1957

> The rumblings of discontent in Asia
> and Africa are expressions of a quest
> for freedom and human dignity. . . .
> So in a real sense the racial crisis in
> America is a part of the larger world
> crisis.
>
> MLK

March 1957: Martin and Coretta King boarded an airplane for their first trip abroad. They joined a delegation of distinguished Americans invited to witness independence ceremonies in Ghana, Britain's former Gold Coast colony in Africa. The invitation to the Kings came from Dr. Kwame Nkrumah, who had led Ghana's drive for freedom from British rule. Dexter and the MIA helped pay travel expenses for the Kings.

King's friendliness and zest for living entertained crew and passengers during the flight. He sat at the controls like a fascinated youngster. "If I just had a few more lessons," he said, "I think I could fly us all to Accra myself."

The jovial mood continued in Accra, Ghana's capital, where the Kings received treatment reserved for heads of government. During one of the ceremonies, Vice President Richard Nixon, the official U.S. representative, walked over to chat with the Montgomery hero. "I recognize you from your picture on the cover of *Time*," Nixon said. "That was a mighty fine story about you." Nixon invited King to come to the White House and confer with him after they returned home.

The high drama of the Ghana celebration came on the evening when fifty thousand Ghanians assembled at the Polo Grounds. Most of them wore the colorful robes of their native tribes. Minutes before midnight on March 5, 1957, the bells of Accra began to ring with joyful sounds. Kwame Nkrumah, tall and regal in the robes of his native village, mounted a platform precisely at the stroke of midnight, and raised his hand toward the sky. The red, white, and blue flag, symbol of colonial dependency, came down. The new green, gold, and red colors of Ghana took its place.

"At long last, the battle is ended," Nkrumah called out. "Ghana, our beloved country, is free forever."

"Freedom, Freedom!" The crowd chanted the words in various tribal languages. "Ghana is free!"

Dr. Nkrumah wept for joy. And King, overcome by the historic significance of the event, shed tears with the Africans. Dark-skinned people, history's exploited underclass, were beginning to awaken to their strength. Martin King identified closely with this Third World movement of "colonial" people for freedom and independence, for American blacks had come to view themselves as African-Americans because of strong ancestral roots in Africa. Before leaving Ghana, the Kings dined privately with Prime Minister Nkrumah, who had studied and taught at American universities. He told King how the Montgomery bus boycott had given him inspiration to continue the protest in Ghana.

In turn, the African experience proved to King the need to quicken the pace of integration in his own country. Early in 1957, a group of Southern black ministers had formed an organization that they named the Southern Christian Leadership Conference (SCLC). As president of SCLC, King planned that the organization would form protest groups across the South, providing a stronger organizational base for launching new programs. The SCLC could then harness the untapped power of the masses of poor blacks.

Power, King decided, was the missing element in the struggle for black equality, in America and elsewhere. In America, power radiated from Washington, D.C. By 1957 he was looking for ways to bring the might of the United States president into the movement for equal rights. This would force other federal and state officials to recognize that American racism had become the number-one American problem.

On his way home from Ghana, King stopped in New York to plan a rally that would send an appeal to Washington officials. He met with the two most influential black leaders in America, men who presented contrasting features and personalities. Roy Wilkins, Executive Director of the NAACP, at fifty-five, was slender and brown-skinned. His trim mustache and suave manner gave him a sophisticated appearance. Wilkins believed in a legalistic approach to combat racial injustices, working through the courts. Asa Philip Randolph, organizer of the all-black Brotherhood of Sleeping Car Porters, was tall and commanding. For years he had urged the use of mass action by blacks to influence federal legislation and court decisions in the battle against racial discrimination and for full equality.

Martin King had now earned the right to join these "big two." He recognized the need for court action; it had played a decisive part in the Montgomery struggle. But he agreed with Randolph that a mass movement, too, was needed to convince Congress of the need for new civil rights legislation.

The last civil rights act to be passed was the Act of 1875, which guaranteed for all races "the full and equal enjoyment of accommodations in inns, theaters . . . and public conveyances on land and water." Almost at once, in 1883, the Supreme Court struck down this act, and declared it to be unconstitutional. The Court's decision was a big step toward Jim Crow.

Now, in 1957, the Justice Department had drafted new civil rights legislation to guarantee the right of equal access for black people to education, housing, and the ballot. To ensure speedy passage of this bill, Randolph believed, the people must speak out. The lawmakers in Washington, D.C. must hear from them.

With this in mind, King, Wilkins, and Randolph outlined plans for a Prayer Pilgrimage to be held in the nation's capital on May 17, 1957, the third anniversary of the Supreme Court's *Brown* decision. The purpose of the pilgrimage, King told an audience, "is to register our protest with Congress, not to make any threats."

The task of organizing the demonstration was given to two civil rights activists known for their skill in organizing mass assemblies: Bayard Rustin and Ella Baker. Rustin was still a key assistant to King, and helped to organize SCLC. Baker, a black woman with a brilliant mind, had devoted her life selflessly to civil rights organizations. Through April and early May Baker and Rustin headed up a corps of workers who planned the pilgrimage. They sent out a letter of invitation to black ministers throughout the South. "Come to Washington on May 17," the letter said, "and bring your congregations with you. We will pray for freedom on the steps of the Lincoln Memorial."

The people came. Governors and mayors of several big states and cities, including New York, declared May 17, 1957, "Pilgrimage Day." Trade unions and other organized groups donated funds for expenses and sent delegations. Pilgrims from distant points came by airplane, others by buses or automobiles. One preacher walked 180 miles from his home in New Jersey.

Shortly before noon on that lovely spring day of May 17, an estimated thirty-seven thousand pilgrims assembled in front of the marble monument to Abraham Lincoln, a favorite gathering place for huge demonstrations of historic significance. Some sat on the two thousand folding chairs. Most stood. The crowd represented thirty-three states. Approximately one out of ten was white. People called out names and pointed as they spotted celebrities. A. Philip Randolph presided and moved the program briskly along, as a parade of speakers and entertainers thrilled the crowd. Each speaker was limited to about ten minutes. Mordecai Johnson, whose lecture on India inspired King, was among them. The program had been going on three hours when an interracial choral group from the Philadelphia Fellowship House performed a musical selection. Before they finished the crowd began to stir. It was obvious that the next speaker was the person most had come to hear. Randolph boomed the introduction: "I give you Martin Luther King!"

Dressed in his flowing clergyman's robe, Reverend King stood before the statue of the Great Emancipator. He began speaking about voting rights, guaranteed by the Fifteenth Amendment. He told the listeners that "so long as I do not firmly and irrevocably possess the right to vote, I do not possess myself."

Martin King made the most of every second in his allotted ten minutes, reminding listeners that votes could be translated into power—the power to chart their own destiny and to choose leaders who would work for the interests of the voters. In the rousing oratorical style of a Baptist preacher, he shifted cadence, voice inflection, and timing, melding listeners and speaker in a rhythmic, syncopated call-and-response cycle. The crowd picked up the chant "give us the ballot," and then waited for King to itemize the benefits voting rights would bring.

"Give us the ballot . . . [*Give us the ballot!*] and we will no longer plead to the Federal government. . . ."

"Give us the ballot . . . [*Give us the ballot!*] and we will fill our legislative halls with men of good will. . . ."

"Give us the ballot . . . [*Give us the ballot!*] and we will place judges on the benches of the South who will do justly and love mercy . . . ."

The crowd kept up the chanting, raising emotional levels higher with each sentence.

"Give us the ballot . . . [*Give us the ballot!*] and we will quietly and nonviolently, without rancor or bitterness implement the Supreme Court decision of May 17, 1954. . . ."

Martin King emerged from the Prayer Pilgrimage as the number-one leader of 16 million black people in the United

States. "At this point in his career," said the *Amsterdam News* of New York City, "the people will follow him anywhere."

That fall, the civil rights bill passed. Success was due largely to Lyndon Baines Johnson, the powerful senator from Texas. He had to make compromises to win votes for passage, and this weakened the bill significantly. Nevertheless, it was a victory, the first civil rights legislation since 1875. The 1957 act established a Civil Rights Division within the Justice Department. It also created a Federal Civil Rights Commission, with authority to investigate the status of civil rights in the United States and to make recommendations for new legislation. In addition, the Justice Department was given authority to intervene in instances when violations of individual civil rights occurred. This included attempts to vote and to register to attend integrated schools.

For the remainder of the year, King continued to travel about the country, giving speeches to inspire white and black listeners to work together for racial harmony. In 1957 alone he traveled 780,000 miles and made over two hundred speeches.

During that year too, King pondered future projects for the newly organized SCLC and for himself. In late 1957 several crises over school desegregation commanded his attention. A generation of black students had moved into their teen years during the Montgomery bus boycott. During their impressionable years, in grade school, these black students had followed the day-to-day happenings. They learned about the incredible courage of King and of everyday folk who walked for freedom. It is understandable, then, that it was a teenage vanguard who kept the civil rights issue in the news headlines during the period King prepared to launch new civil rights projects.

The issue was school integration. Southern Congressmen urged citizens to resist it. Segregationists formed new hate groups to frighten blacks who dared to try and enroll in white schools. The best known, the Citizens' Council, was composed chiefly of middle-class whites and called itself the "white-collar Klan." It even patterned its actions after the Ku Klux Klan, which formed in 1866 when laws were being passed to give civil rights to ex-slaves. Black parents who tried to enroll their children in all-white schools faced a range of retributions, from threatening telephone calls to death. But the black teenagers stunned the world by their courage and determination to implement the Supreme Court *Brown* decision.

This courage made nine students in Little Rock, Arkansas the center of world attention. Arkansas and Texas were the only two Southern states working to comply with the *Brown* decision. Little Rock's school board decided to begin with limited integration in one school—Central High—admitting only a few students. Other schools would be integrated over a six-year period.

Segregationists mounted opposition to any school integration. Many politicians gained overnight popularity by encouraging their defiance. Nevertheless, seventy-five black students signed for enrollment in Central High. The school board screened the list to twenty-five, then began calling parents of these finalists to dissuade them from enrolling. If there must be integration, they wanted as few black students as possible. In the end, only nine black students remained candidates, three boys and six girls. The president of the Arkansas NAACP, Mrs. Daisy Bates, volunteered to counsel them. A well-known activist, Mrs. Bates and her husband owned and published a black newspaper, the *State Star*.

Daisy Bates knew beforehand that she, and the students, faced danger. In her book, *The Long Shadow of Little Rock,* she tells of the night a rock crashed through her living room window. "I reached for the rock lying in the middle of the floor. A note was tied to it . . . scrawled in bold print were the words . . . 'stone this time, dynamite next.'" Despite such threats, Bates helped the nine students prepare for school integration.

The night before school opened, Arkansas Governor Orville Faubus spoke on statewide public television. He planned to run for reelection to a third term, so he told the white listeners what he knew they wanted to hear. For the time being, he announced, the schools "must be operated on

the same basis as they have operated in the past. . . ."
Furthermore, he said, National Guardsmen were being
ordered to surround Central High. Listeners knew the troops
were being sent, not only to keep order outside, but to keep
the nine black students from going inside the school.

Daisy Bates drove by Central High that night and later
described the sight. "Under the street lights stretched a long
line of army trucks with canvas tops. Men in full battle
dress—helmets, boots and bayonets—were piling out of the
trucks and lining up in front of the school."

"What's going to happen?" the black students questioned
Mrs. Bates. Nobody really knew. Rumors circulated that
caravans of white supremacists from all over the state were
headed for Little Rock to keep the black students from going
into the school. Governor Faubus then declared Central High
off limits to blacks. He offered a chilling prediction. If black
students attempted to enter the school, he said, "blood would
run in the streets."

The American public followed the sequence. The students
became known as "The Little Rock Nine." Daisy Bates began
calling local ministers, black and white, and a few agreed to
escort the Nine on their first school day. The school superintendent had asked parents of the nine students not to
accompany their children, thinking the sight of black adults
might incite any crowd that gathered. The police department
promised Mrs. Bates limited help. "The school is considered
off limits to the city police while it is 'occupied' by the
Arkansas National Guardsmen," a spokesman said.

On September 3, Daisy Bates telephoned the parents to let
them know about the ministers and to give instructions where
the students should meet. By the time she made the last call it
was 3 A.M. Suddenly, Daisy Bates had a nightmarish thought.
She had not sent a message to the parents of Elizabeth
Eckford, one of the Nine. The girl's family had no telephone.
Mrs. Bates decided to meet Elizabeth early the next morning.

Elizabeth Eckford, a strong-willed fifteen-year-old, later
explained how she anticipated her first day of integrated

schooling. "That night I was so excited I couldn't sleep. The next morning I was about the first one up . . ."

She tried to comfort her parents as they listened to newscasters who questioned whether black students would dare show up at the school. Her father paced the floor, too nervous to smoke either the pipe in one hand, or the cigarette in the other. Before Elizabeth left, the family went into the living room and prayed together. "Don't worry," she comforted them.

On that Wednesday, September 4, the slender, curly-haired teenager, wearing the white-and-black plaid dress she and her mother had made for the occasion, left for school. The eyes behind the frame glasses looked straight ahead. Her right arm swung rhythmically as she walked while her left hand cradled her books. She took the public bus—a little too soon.

As Daisy Bates drove to try and get to the school ahead of Elizabeth, her car radio suddenly announced a bulletin: "A Negro girl is being mobbed at Central High . . ." Elizabeth Eckford faced the mob alone. "Here she comes," someone called. "Get ready."

The school girl later described that morning when she expected a National Guardsman to help her. "I didn't know what to do . . . When I tried to squeeze past him, he raised his bayonet, and then the other guards moved in and raised their bayonets."

Somebody started yelling, "Lynch her! Lynch her!" The guards watched, but made no attempt to help the girl. "I looked into the face of an old woman," she remembered, "and it seemed a kind face, but when I looked at her again, she spat on me." Elizabeth looked down the block and saw a bench at the bus stop. "If I can get there, I will be safe," she reasoned. She ran to the bench and sat down. A part of the crowd ran after her, calling for a lynching. "Drag her over to a tree."

Dr. Benjamin Fine, *New York Times* education editor, walked over to the trembling girl, put his arm around her, and raised her chin. "Don't let them see you cry," he said gently. A white woman, Grace Larch, joined them and turned to the

Elizabeth Ann Eckford tries to pass hecklers and National Guardsmen to enter Central High School in Little Rock, Arkansas. After graduating from Central High and Central State College Ms. Eckford served in the U.S. Army and then returned to Little Rock, where she still resides. (UPI/Bettman Newsphotos)

mob. "Leave the child alone," she commanded. She rode the bus with Elizabeth and saw her safely home.

The other eight students, two ministers in front, two behind, approached the school. Guardsmen stopped them on orders from the governor. No black student entered Central High that day. However, they had precipitated a test of state versus federal authority. Governor Faubus kept the Arkansas National Guard stationed around the school. A crowd of segregationists came daily to stand watch. Daisy Bates and the nine students refused to give up. A team of NAACP lawyers, including Thurgood Marshall, appealed to the federal court. A district judge issued court orders, forbidding Faubus from interfering with school integration. The governor withdrew the guards and left the state for a conference.

An unruly mob replaced the guards and surrounded Central High. On September 23, the students assembled at the Bates home, waiting for police officers who took them into the school through a side delivery entrance. When the crowd learned this, they threatened to storm the building.

"Let's go get our shotguns," one man called out. "I hope they drag nine dead niggers out," cried another. "Don't stay in there with them," agitators yelled to students inside. White students ran out to swell the crowd that became larger and louder every hour. Near noon, the black students were summoned to the principal's office. He was sending them home, the principal said, because he could not guarantee their safety. The police commander arrived and quickly took the nine students from the building and drove them home.

The "Little Rock Crisis" dominated front-page news nationally and internationally. Letters and telegrams from all over the world descended on Governor Faubus, school officials, and local newspapers. Mail also came to the youngsters who had taken a stand as brave as the adult boycotters in Montgomery. The picture of Elizabeth Eckford, facing a burly Guardsman, and the hate-etched faces of the mob, was publicized and became a symbol of the antiracist, antiapartheid cause. Millions of eyes were watching!

President Eisenhower knew it. The school integration crisis had forced a confrontation between state and federal government. The president issued an emergency proclamation to make his position clear: The law and the orders of the federal court must be obeyed. He ordered "all persons engaged in such obstruction of justice to cease and desist therefrom, and to disperse. . . ."

On Tuesday, September 24, the president spoke on radio and television, saying, "I have today issued an executive order directing the use of troops . . . at Little Rock, Arkansas . . .

Thus will be restored," he said, "the image of America and all its parts, as one nation, indivisible, with liberty and justice for all."

These were historic words. For the first time since the Reconstruction era, federal troops were sent to the South to protect the rights of black people. For leaders of the black struggle, this meant that the executive powers of the president could play a major part in securing civil rights. As for segregationists, the federal intervention intensified their bitterness toward blacks and solidified their resistance.

For the Nine, it meant another chance to integrate a Southern school. "Will the children be going to Central High tomorrow?" news reporters asked Daisy Bates. Only the Nine could answer. The parents were against sending their children to face the dangers again, but the young people wanted to go. A school official called to ask Daisy Bates which of the children were at her house to be taken to school. "All nine," she answered firmly.

The night before the students were to return to school, two white ministers visited each of their homes and prayed with the families. The next morning a convoy rolled up to the Bates' home, jeeps with machine-gun mounts to lead and follow the van carrying the students. The paratrooper in charge saluted and spoke formally. "Mrs. Bates, we're ready for the children. We will return them to your home at three-thirty o'clock."

Minnijean Brown, one of the nine, said, "For the first time in my life, I feel like an American citizen."

September 25, 1957, the nine black students passed through the front door of Central High, guarded by soldiers. Around the building paratroopers stood at attention. Inside the school, each of the nine was escorted by a personal military guard.

Despite protection, the Nine knew they would need much courage to stay in Central High. They braved kicks, name-calling, trippings, thrown objects, spitting, and more. Being young, they could see hopeful signs. The school paper, the *Tiger,* printed a challenge to all Central High students. "The challenge is yours, as future adults of America, to prove your maturity, intelligence and ability to make decisions by how you react, behave and conduct yourselves on this controversial question. What is your answer to this challenge?"

The answer was change and eventual understanding. The progress, though slow, was due largely to the courage of the Little Rock Nine. They won the admiration of well-wishers in countries they had never thought of. The volume of mail kept their spirits high. One of the girls said: "I take letters with me to school; they make you feel good, people sharing things with you. I read them in school." Another student said: "I read a letter every morning before I go to school, and it makes me feel good all day, and I read one when I come back. It lifts my spirit."

On graduation day, May 29, 1958, Ernest Green joined his 601 white classmates as the seniors received diplomas. The seventeen-year-old reflected, "I figured I was making a statement. . . . I knew that once I got as far as that principal and received the diploma, I had cracked the wall."

4

"STRIDE TOWARD FREEDOM" AND A PILGRIMAGE TO INDIA, 1958-1959

> Nonviolent resistance . . . is based on the conviction that the universe is on the side of justice. Consequently the believer in nonviolence has deep faith in the future.
>
> MLK

"Let us make our intentions crystal clear. We want freedom—now. We do not want freedom fed to us in teaspoonfuls over another one hundred years." With such hard-hitting speeches, Martin King kicked off the Crusade for Citizenship in 1958. His goal was to double black voters in two years.

Another immediate goal was to involve the president in the civil rights movement. After a series of insistent telegrams from SCLC, Eisenhower agreed to meet with selected leaders. On Monday, June 23, the group assembled in the Oval Office of the White House. It included Martin King, Ralph Abernathy, Roy Wilkins, A. Philip Randolph, and Lester B. Granger, the sixty-one-year-old executive secretary of the Urban League. The leaders presented a nine-point statement of action that the president could take to inform Americans that "the law will be vigorously upheld with the total resources at [my] command."

Eisenhower listened politely but he made no specific promises. The meeting was a breakthrough, however. A copy of the nine-point statement was left with the chief executive and another was given to the press. The world would know that Eisenhower had been advised—and warned. Also, pictures of the black leaders and the president on the front page of the *New York Times* gave black people pride and hope.

That summer the Atlanta SCLC office began to function vigorously with the coming of Ella Baker. The super-organizer had come to set up the office for King but stayed on to coordinate activities and hire a staff. The lone woman in a minister-dominated organization, the strong, smart, hard-working, and experienced Ella Baker held her own. She brought in people who helped shape SCLC into a force for change. Her coming was due largely to one of King's loyal friends, Stanley D. Levison, a wealthy white New York attorney who had raised money for the Montgomery bus boycott. He continued to support all of King's projects.

Martin King's major project for the summer of 1958 was the completion of the manuscript for a book about the Montgomery story. The protest had inspired similar movements in scores of other cities, and a book about the courageous people who "walked for freedom" could inspire still others. Dr. Lawrence Dunbar Reddick, a historian who took part in the boycott, helped with research. At the same time Reddick began a full-length biography of King. Harper & Row contracted to publish both books.

With constant interruptions at home, King finally rented a room in an Atlanta hotel to finish the manuscript. One night as he worked there he stopped to answer a knock at his door. There stood James Baldwin, the gifted black novelist, his large expressive eyes surveying King and the desk covered with manuscript pages. Baldwin, like King, was fighting so-cial evils, but he did so through his novels and essays. The two men soon formed a close friendship. Baldwin later visited Montgomery and Dexter to observe King with the people. In *Harper's* magazine, he explained why King made a great leader. "The secret of his greatness," Baldwin said in part, "does not lie in his voice or his presence or his manner, though it has something to do with all these. . . . The secret lies, I

think, in his intimate knowledge of the people he is address-
ing, be they black or white, and in the forthrightness with
which he speaks of those things which hurt and baffle them."

With the major editing of his book completed, assisted in
the final stage by his two friends, Bayard Rustin and Stanley
Levison, King could relax a bit. On September 3, he and
Coretta went to support Abernathy in court, where he was
scheduled to testify against a man who had assaulted him. As
the Kings tried to enter the Montgomery County courtroom,
a surly guard blocked their way. King asked to speak with
Abernathy's lawyer, and the guards became furious. "Boy,
you done done it now" one shouted. "Let's go!" They twisted
King's arms behind his back in a hammerlock, pushed him
down the steps and around the corner to the police station. As
officers frisked him, one grabbed him by the throat, and when
they shoved him into a cell, both policemen gave him a few
kicks. Later, when the police commissioner found out that the
prisoner was the famous citizen recently pictured on the cover
of *Time* magazine, he immediately released King on bond.

That night Martin and Coretta King talked a long time
about the incident. "If I commit a crime in the name of civil
rights," King decided, "I will go to jail and serve the time."
Thoreau, he recalled, had gone to jail for his civil disobedience. Gandhi willingly spent years in jail during the long
campaign for India's independence.

At King's trial, the judge sentenced him to fourteen days in
jail or pay a fine. King asked to make a statement, the way
Gandhi often did before he went to jail. "I could not in all conscience pay a fine for an act I did not commit and above all for
brutal treatment that I did not deserve . . .," King added,
"Something must happen to awaken the dozing conscience of
America before it is too late. The time has come when perhaps
only the willing and nonviolent acts of suffering by the innocent can arouse the nation. . . ." The police commissioner,
attempting to stem the outcry over King's jailing, quietly paid
the fine and King was forced to leave.

That night he spoke to the welcoming crowd at a mass
meeting. "When one of you goes to jail and suffers brutality,

no one knows about it," he told them. "I am happy that I could suffer just a little bit. . . . It makes me feel a closer part of you." The experience caused King to meditate more about the problems faced by the poor, undereducated, defenseless blacks who were at the mercy of white society. He had never been truly poor. Even during the bus boycott, he had not been unprotected. That night King moved to a closer empathy with the underclass of American society.

Younger than most national leaders, he also identified closely with America's young people. School integration had thrust many of them into the movement for equal rights. When A. Philip Randolph began planning a Youth March for Integrated Schools, King was elated to become honorary chairman and keynote speaker. They planned the March for October 25.

Before then, however, King's book had to be publicized. *Stride Toward Freedom: The Montgomery Story* reached bookstores in September 1958. King began a series of promotional appearances. An autographing session was scheduled in Blumstein's department store in Harlem for September 20. Most of Harlem's residents were black or Puerto Rican, many living in crowded conditions. Laws did not dictate racial separation, but poverty and housing patterns did. Living conditions made the potential for violence ever-present.

That Saturday King sat at a desk in a section of Blumstein's set up for the book sales. Book buyers waited patiently in line for the author to sign their copies. King smiled and chatted in his personable manner.

Without warning the scene changed. A middle-aged, well-dressed black woman pushed her way through the crowd. "Is this Martin Luther King?" she asked, leaning over the desk.

"Yes, it is." King smiled a friendly greeting.

Suddenly in one swift motion the woman raised a shiny letter-opener and stabbed the sharp point into King's chest. She then began beating him with her fist and ranting in a crazed manner. Horrified onlookers grabbed the woman and held her until security officers came. Photographers took pictures. A bystander rushed to pull the weapon from King's

Dr. King sits calmly, the letter-opener protruding from his chest, following his stabbing during an autographing session in a New York department store. (New York Daily News)

chest, but someone warned, "Don't touch it!" From a distance the wail of sirens announced an ambulance.

Amid the commotion King sat absolutely motionless. The letter-opener protruded from his upper left chest. If the blade tip rested near his heart or major artery, any motion could bring sudden death. He kept this composure during the ambulance ride to Harlem Hospital, the weapon still in his chest. An interracial team of surgeons removed the weapon, which was eight inches in length. Doctors told King later that the tip rested against the outer wall of the aorta. "If you had sneezed during all those hours of waiting," they explained, "your aorta would have punctured and you would have drowned in your own blood."

Radio and television programming paused to let the world know that Dr. Martin Luther King, Jr. lay critically ill. Announcers repeated the bulletins the way they do in a national emergency. Thousands of well-wishers began a vigil outside the hospital, singing and praying for King's recovery. Even people who had paid scant attention to King's work before began to discuss what he was saying about racial harmony and equal justice for everyone.

In Montgomery, Coretta's composure was as steely as her husband's. She arranged for the care of their children, then immediately took a plane for New York, accompanied by Abernathy and King's sister, Christine. His parents followed soon after. The hospital thoughtfully set up an office where Coretta could handle the avalanche of mail and gifts and offers of help. As her husband began to recover, he was cheered by the letters, especially those from children. A note from a white writer reminded him, "Your voice is the only true voice of love today, and we hear. . . ."

King's belief in nonviolence extended to the woman who nearly killed him, identified as Mrs. Izola Curry. "Don't prosecute her, get her healed," he advised authorities. Examinations proved her mentally ill, and she was placed in a state hospital.

As he continued his recovery, King and his wife talked at length about the future. Coretta recalled, "It was as if both of us knew that this was not the time—that this trial was preparing us for something that was still to come."

With this faith, they returned to Montgomery on October 24. The Youth March for Integrated Schools was scheduled the next day, but King was too weak to take part. Coretta stood in for him. On that fall day of clear blue skies, around ten thousand demonstrators marched down Constitution Avenue toward the Lincoln Memorial. Some marchers were as young as fourth graders. The majority were college students. The placards they hoisted high publicized the organizations that sponsored their trip to Washington— NAACP Youth Councils, labor groups, church clubs. Leading them all was the man known as Mr. Civil Rights: Asa Philip Randolph. Other black dignitaries walked with him. Coretta, wearing her hair in the popular shoulder-length style, looked as young and pretty as though she were one of the college students.

From the steps of the Lincoln Memorial, adult and student speakers brought the issue of school integration before the American public. A delegation of twelve students, accompanied by Harry Belafonte, went to the gates of the White House to deliver a petition on school integration. They were denied entrance to the grounds, but their petition was finally forwarded to the presidential press secretary. The entire delegation of students adopted a resolution calling for a second Youth March the following April.

In Montgomery, King continued his slow recovery. The enforced rest period, with all appointments canceled, seemed a perfect time to accept a long-standing invitation from the Gandhi National Memorial Fund to visit India. The American Friends Services Committee, a Quaker organization, gave a grant for travel expenses. SCLC also gave a gift of money.

In early February 1959, Martin and Coretta King left for India. Lawrence Reddick, who had completed the King biography, accompanied them. A welcoming crowd met them in New Delhi, India's capital. As the Americans stood with their shoulders heaped with garlands of flowers, reporters crowded around to ask questions. "To other countries I may go as a tourist," King told them, "but to India I come as a pilgrim. This is because India means to me Mahatma Gandhi, a truly great man of the ages." When reporters asked about the Montgomery bus boycott, King said: "Our victory is not so much in the desegregation of the buses, as it is a new sense of dignity and destiny."

After a tea, and then a reception, the Americans passed through the high wrought-iron gates leading to the residence of Jawaharlal Nehru, the first Indian to become prime minister. Handsome in white fitted trousers and long white coat with a red rose pinned on it, Nehru greeted the visitors in genuine friendship. "I've read so much about Gandhi and the source of the nonviolent movement here," King told his host, "that I wanted to come and see for myself."

He was surprised to know how much the prime minister already knew about him. For four hours the two leaders talked about the similarity between the struggle in India to end racial and religious intolerance and the struggle in America to end racial segregation and injustices. Nehru explained that he was working to end the "caste" system. There was a class—or "caste," as they called it, of poor people in India, the lowest of the low, who did all the hard and dirty work. They were called "Untouchables," which meant that they were victims of an Indian Jim Crow system. Nehru told Martin King that the government was struggling to end this type of discrimination. Untouchables were now being offered special privileges to help right the wrongs that they had suffered.

Reddick asked an interesting question. Was special preference not a form of discrimination?

"Well, it may be," Nehru answered, "but this is our way of atoning for the centuries of injustice we have inflicted upon these people." Martin King took note. Perhaps there should be similar programs of compensation for black Americans to make up for past injustices and lack of opportunities.

Before breakfast the next morning, the American pilgrims visited Gandhi's *Samadhi,* the shrine in the place where he was cremated after his assassination in 1948. In the exquisite garden the Kings placed a wreath at the memorial and knelt for a time in prayer.

Over the next days they began a journey that carried them around the coast of India. They traveled by train, plane, truck, and jeep to cover the varied terrain. Some days they visited large cities. Other times they tramped the dusty roads of rural villages. They visited a village of Untouchables. The poverty there, as in other villages, was heartbreaking. Another day they had lunch with poor people and ate the way millions of Indians did, seated on the ground and using banana leaves for dishes.

They watched the poor people, dressed in rags and carrying the pitiful items they owned wrapped together. At night they slept on sidewalks, for they had no homes, and during the day they rummaged through garbage cans for food. After the trip

King talked of this lack of food and the high cost of storing grain in America. "I know where we can store it free of charge," he said, "in the wrinkled stomachs of starving people in Asia and Africa."

The trip included other unforgettable experiences. As the Montgomery boycott hero walked village streets, Indian children warmed to his infectious smile and clamored to hold his hands. There were other occasions when he addressed large audiences in cities and talked about the Montgomery protest. Coretta usually sang as part of these programs. Dressed in a colorful sari, the free-flowing garment of long cloth worn by Indian women, she sang the old American spirituals that the Indians loved to hear. King said later, "Coretta sang as much as I lectured."

Perhaps the most beneficial moments of the trip were the times King engaged in long walks with people who had worked with Gandhi. He learned about Gandhi's work in South Africa as a young man fresh out of law school in London. Gandhi went there to work for twelve months, and stayed twenty-one years, trying to remedy the discrimination and abuse against dark-skinned people by the British, who controlled South Africa. He led many campaigns for the rights of Indians in South Africa and experimented with his method of nonviolent action, which he called *satyagraha,* "force born of love and truth." Gandhi and his followers suffered imprisonment, hunger, and assaults by lawmen, but in the end won some of their rights.

In 1915, Gandhi returned to India and mounted *satyagraha* campaigns to end British domination of India and unfair laws and taxes that kept the people in extreme poverty. Gandhi's followers described for King the phases of these campaigns. The first step was sincere negotiation. If this failed, a sequence of action would follow:

· Preparation for direct action
· Agitation and excitement—mass meetings, rallies, etc.
· An ultimatum
· Boycotts and strikes

- Noncooperation and civil disobedience
- Assertive *satyagraha*—usurpation of the functions of government
- Establishment of a government to oppose the established regime.

Martin King ruled out the last two stages, but kept in mind the other steps for future civil rights campaigns. He was deeply impressed by the way the spirit of Gandhi was still alive in India, even though the saintly leader had been dead for ten years. Photographs and statues showed the frail Mahatma, "Great Soul," dressed in the white homespun cloth worn by peasants. He was often pictured walking along the countryside and stopping to talk with children.

A reminder of King's first introduction to Gandhi came when he visited the "abode of peace," the ashram, or religious community, of the renown Indian poet Rabindranath Tagore. It was there that Mordecai Johnson had attended the World Pacifist Conference that student King heard about in his lecture. Poet Tagore wrote lines about Gandhi that could give any world leader hope:

> Perhaps he will fail as the Buddha failed and as Christ failed to wean men from their iniquities, but he will always be remembered as one who made his life a lesson for all ages to come.

The pilgrimage to India proved to be a landmark in King's life, moving him closer to the leadership role he felt destined to play. Coretta wrote later, "Martin returned from India more devoted than ever to Gandhian ideals of nonviolence and simplicity of living." She also noted, "One thing he learned was patience. It had taken nearly half a century for the Indian people to gain their independence."

King began to shape plans for future civil rights projects, which he saw as an extension of his Christian ministry. These plans included America's youth. On April 18, he proudly led the second Youth March on Washington. Publicity over his appearance brought two and a half times the number of the first March. In his keynote address King emphasized the importance of voting, a recurring theme in his speeches. Two of the other main speakers were Roy Wilkins of the NAACP, and Tom Mboya, leader of Kenya, in East Africa. At least eleven African nations would gain independence within a year.

As before, a delegation of students went to the White House. This time a presidential assistant met them and gave assurance that Eisenhower shared their determination to end racial discrimination.

King set out to make sure that the president kept his word. By the fall of 1958 he had melded Gandhi's philosophy of *satyagraha,* Thoreau's theory of civil disobedience, and his own belief in Christianity as the foundation of love. He shaped a philosophy of nonviolent direct action he called, "the most potent weapon available to an oppressed people in the struggle for freedom." By the close of 1959 he was ready to test it. He had faith in the goodness of his fellow Americans, Northern and Southern. "This is a daring faith," he concluded, "but I choose to invest my life in it."

He needed time, as well as a broader base for operating. After weeks of agonizing over the decision, he submitted his resignation to his beloved Dexter congregation on the last Sunday in November. "I can't stop now," he told them. "History has thrust something upon me which I cannot turn away. . . ." In sadness, Dexter released their pastor for a higher calling destiny seemed to have in store for him. As they linked hands and sang their favorite hymn, "Blest Be the Tie That Binds," pastor and people wept together. Tears were as much for the joy of having known each other as for the sorrow of parting.

The next day King issued a statement: "The time has come for a bold, broad advance of the Southern campaign for equality. . . ." These plans included roles for America's youth. "We must train our youth and adult leaders in the techniques of social change through nonviolent resistance. We must employ new methods of struggle involving the masses of the people."

Young people had already become attuned to King's dream of the true America, as set forth in the Declaration of Independence. The generation that matured during the years following the *Brown* court decision had become accustomed to change. In an electronic age they did not have to wait for historic changes to be printed, then learned. They watched history in the making. They saw a young black minister-scholar stand up to racists and direct a drama that gripped the world for a full year. They saw students like Elizabeth Eckford face insults and possible death daily as they integrated schools. And lively televised newscasts showed how the once-dominated African nations were gaining independence.

Impressionable, idealistic black students became fascinated with the concept of nonviolent action. In the late 1950s King found a black graduate student who was eager to teach it. His name was James Lawson. A ruggedly handsome young man who looked at the world through his horned-rimmed glasses with kind eyes, Lawson believed firmly in pacifism. He chose to go to jail rather than fight in the Korean War. A group of ministers helped him to go to India later and spend his time as a missionary working with poor people. During his three years in India Lawson learned about Gandhi's campaigns and his methods. He returned home and learned about the Montgomery bus boycott that used Gandhi's nonviolent tactics, and went to talk with King. When the two met again while King was speaking at Oberlin College and Lawson was studying there, King encouraged him to spread the ideals of nonviolence throughout the civil rights movement. When the Fellowship of Reconciliation (FOR) opened a regional office in Nashville, Lawson joined the staff and transferred to the divinity school of Vanderbilt University. He teamed up with Glenn Smiley, who helped King during the Montgomery protest, to begin holding workshops on nonviolence in Nashville. Lawson also visited other colleges in the South. By the close of 1959, many black students in the South had at least heard of these workshops.

In Nashville, students crowded the sessions as though they were college courses for special credits. As part of their workshops, the black college students began what they called "testing the lunch counters." Small groups asked to be served in department store restaurants and were refused. The students made plans to expand this testing after the Christmas holidays of 1959 and to involve larger groups.

So it was that at the threshold of the sixties, in a nation where most adult leaders were floundering with traditional solutions to old problems, black college students took center stage. The Youth Movement caught the nation by surprise.

5

THE SIT-INS, 1960

A generation of young people experienced the majestic dignity of a
direct struggle for its own liberation.
MLK

On the last day of January 1960, seventeen-year-old
Joseph McNeil entered the lunch counter in the bus station of Greensboro, North Carolina. "I'd like a
hamburger and a cup of coffee," he said.

The white waitress looked at the brown-skinned, well-
attired college student and answered with four familiar,
dehumanizing words: "We don't serve Negroes."

That Sunday night in the dormitory of Greenboro's
Agricultural and Technical College, known as A & T, McNeil
fumed over the incident with friends. His roommate, Izell
Blair, and two buddies, Franklin McCain and David
Richmond, shared his indignation. All were freshmen. All
were seventeen except McCain, who was eighteen. And all
had been members of the NAACP Youth Council. Each night
after their studies, the four friends usually engaged in a lively
"bull session," discussing topics of interest to them. That
night they talked about segregation. "We've talked long
enough," one said, "Let's do something."

Next day, wearing coats and ties, they strolled into the F.
W. Woolworth store on Elm Street. They purchased several

personal articles and school supplies, asking casually for receipts.

The store clock registered 4:30.

Next, the students walked to the L-shaped lunch counter, took seats, and ordered coffee. The waitress gave the predictable answer. "I'm sorry, but we do not serve colored here."

"I beg your pardon," McCain said. "You just served me at a counter two feet away."

The students continued to sit. Shoppers gathered and gaped. A black dishwasher, fearing for the students' safety, came from the kitchen to scold them. A white policeman walked in from the street and paced up and down behind the four, knocking his club against his hand in a show of force. Two old white ladies watched, then came over and gave each student a pat on the shoulder, whispering, "Ah! You should have done it ten years ago." A larger group of whites sneered in disgust. "Nasty niggers!"

The store manager finally appeared. "Why don't you go back to your campus?" he suggested.

By then, as the students described, they had gained "the confidence of a Mack truck." They sat at the counter until the 5:30 closing.

They still did not know whether they would be arrested or beaten when they left the store. What they knew for certain was the lesson of the Montgomery story: Courageous action by a few can spark a revolutionary response from others. The four young men stood in front of Woolworth's, locked their fingers together, and raised their hands toward the heavens to form a pyramid. In hushed voices they recited the Lord's Prayer. They had challenged the Jim Crow System and survived.

That evening they were among the fifty students who gathered in a dormitory room and formed the Student Executive Committee for Justice. The group voted to continue sitting at the lunch counter.

Like students in several Southern black colleges, many of the young people had read an inexpensive booklet published by the Fellowship of Reconciliation titled *Martin Luther King and the Montgomery Story*. The booklet explained the philosophy of nonviolent resistence to unjust practices. The A&T committee agreed to adopt the code of behavior used when the Montgomery buses became integrated.

The sit-in movement began.

More than twenty students returned to Elm Street the next morning and sat at the lunch counter. When they were refused service, they opened their books and began studying. A news service printed the story and told how the well-dressed students ended their sit-in with a prayer. Over the next few days the numbers grew larger each day. The black students were joined by white students from nearby North Carolina College for Women and black women from local Bennett College. By the end of the week, hundreds had joined the protest.

The North Carolina students telephoned and wrote friends at schools in other cities. "Why aren't you doing it?" they asked. Accounts carried by wire services publicized the happenings. Ella Baker, who had joined the staff of SCLC as executive secretary, began telephoning friends on college campuses and contacts in church groups. "What are you going to do?" she prodded them. "It's time to move." Other adult activists began telephoning and organizing networks of support. "Can you start?" they urged. "Are you ready?"

They were ready. With the speed and power of a Silver Meteor express the sit-ins moved southward, gaining momentum along the way. Their activism was encouraged by young black ministers. When the Greensboro sit-ins started, many of them began organizing centers for training students in nonviolent direct action. Most of the ministers were part of SCLC, and that organization played a pivotal role in the spread of the sit-in movement. So did the black churches. It was often in the churches that students were trained and offered space for large meetings.

On February 16, King arrived in Durham to meet with student representatives from North Carolina colleges. He advised them to form a coordinating group, with representatives from area colleges, to direct sit-in activities. He also encouraged them to work toward bringing adults into the sit-in movement.

That night, people filled the White Rock Baptist Church and its courtyard to listen to King speak. "You have the full weight of SCLC behind you in your struggle," he promised. He reminded his listeners that they stood at a crucial point in the freedom movement, and inspired them with lessons he had learned from the Montgomery protest. "At a certain point in every struggle of great importance," he cautioned, "a moment of doubt or hesitation develops." Doubts must never stop them, he advised. "If there is one lesson experience has taught us . . . it is that when you have found by the help of God a correct course, a morally sound objective, you do not equivocate, you do not retreat—you struggle to win a victory." The true objective, King reminded the students, went beyond lunch counter integration. Ultimately, it was personal freedom, "necessary for one's selfhood, one's intrinsic worth."

The sit-ins on various college campuses developed individual characteristics and leadership styles. Most of the sit-in leaders were already campus leaders, with wide contacts and some administrative skills. In Nashville, two of the outstanding leaders were divinity students. Both John Lewis and James Bevel became staunch believers in the philosophy of nonviolent direct action. Two of the other strongest leaders, Diane Nash and Marion Barry, attended Fisk University, founded the year after the Civil War with help from the Freedmen's Bureau.

On February 13, the Nashville sit-in began in earnest. John Lewis later talked about how carefully they dressed. "It was like going to church. You put on your church-going clothes."

Students' behavior was as impeccable as their dress. James Lawson outlined basic codes that were adapted by most of the student protest groups. "Don't curse back if cursed or abused. Show yourselves courteous and friendly at all times. Sit straight and always face the counter. Don't laugh out. Remember love and nonviolence. May God bless each of you.

Remember the teachings of Jesus, Gandhi, and Martin Luther King."

News reporters publicized the strict self-discipline. Editors of *Motive* magazine wrote: "Even when hostile white youths pull hair and snuff out burning cigarettes on the backs of Negro girls, the girls do not retaliate. They pray."

The steely poise sometimes infuriated hecklers. One day as a girl sat in Gandhi-like quietness at a lunch counter, a white man, bent on ruffling her calm, crept up behind her and ground a lighted cigarette into her hair. In elegant slow motion the girl turned her brown face toward her tormentor, flashed a friendly greeting with her eyes—and smiled. Confounded, the man moved on.

Even police arrests failed to intimidate demonstrators. A white student described the day when police arrested them. "The police said 'everybody under arrest,' so we all got up and marched to the wagon. Then they turned around and looked at the counter again, and the second wave of students had taken seats . . . then a third wave. No matter what they did and how many they arrested, there was still a lunch counter full of students there."

News stories from other cities described similar determination. In Orangeburg, South Carolina, college students became inspired after reading *Stride Toward Freedom* by King, and *Rules for Action* by CORE. One thousand students marched through the streets on March 1, holding up bold signs:

> DOWN WITH JIM CROW!
> SEGREGATION IS OBSOLETE!
> ALL SIT OR ALL STAND!

Two weeks later, despite freezing temperatures, five hundred students staged another march. Police drenched them with streams of water from high-pressure hoses, then took them to jail. When city and county jails were filled, the remaining students were herded into an open stockade as though they were cattle. Wet and shivering, the determined protesters sang and prayed. Their movement continued.

In Atlanta, sit-ins started at Morehouse. Julian Bond was a frail, handsome scholar who aspired to be a journalist and poet. Lonnie King was a husky star on the Morehouse football team. The two friends read the news article about the Greensboro sit-in.

"Don't you think it should happen here?" Lonnie King asked.

"It probably will," Julian Bond answered.

It did happen. The March 9 edition of Atlanta's three daily newspapers carried a full-page advertisement titled: "An Appeal to Human Rights." The student manifesto was signed by six representatives, one from each of the adjoining campuses that make up the Atlanta University system.

The appeal hailed the Greensboro sit-in and called for action in Atlanta.

"Every normal human being wants to walk the earth with dignity and abhors any and all proscriptions placed upon him because of race and color. In essence, this is the meaning of the sit-down protests that are sweeping the nation today."

The students left no doubt about their seriousness. "We must say in all candor that we plan to use every legal and nonviolent means at our disposal to secure full citizenship rights of this great democracy of ours."

Shortly afterward students carried out a well-organized sit-in at lunch counters and restaurants in city and state office buildings. Managers not only refused them service but called the police. A paddy wagon took them to jail. Julian Bond voiced the fears of students who had never dreamed of arrests or jails. "I was indicted on enough charges to put me away for ninety-nine years, and you think I wasn't scared?" After more than six hours in jail the students were released.

Martin King encouraged the Atlanta movement, but during this period he had troubles of another kind. In February two local deputies arrived at his home with a warrant for his arrest so that he could be taken back to Alabama to face criminal charges. A Montgomery grand jury had charged him with perjury for deliberately not reporting all income on his 1956 and 1958 state tax returns.

This threat to King's reputation brought deep depression. "Many people will think I am guilty," he told Coretta. He worried that federal prosecution might reduce his effectiveness in the civil rights movement. The only sure way to clear his name would be to win the tax case. But how could he, of all blacks, hope to win in an Alabama court?

Friends and family members rallied to help. Rosa Parks, realizing how King was brooding over the court case, wrote a note to comfort him. In his reply King showed his uncustomary frustration during this period. "In the midst of constant harassment and intimidation because of my involvement in the civil rights struggle," he said, "I often find myself asking, 'Is it worth it?' But then a friend of good will comes along with kind and encouraging words that give me renewed vigor and courage to carry on."

Other friends of good will, headed by Harry Belafonte, Stanley Levison and Bayard Rustin, formed a committee to raise money for legal defense. King confided to close friends that this effort might divert donations needed for SCLC and the student movement. He could understand why several black leaders criticized the committee's purpose. "In the long run of history," King said, "it does not matter whether Martin Luther King spends ten years in jail, but it does matter whether the movement continues and it does matter whether the Negro is able to get the ballot in the South." At his insistence, his friends included other programs in their fund drive.

A true test of King's courage was his return to Montgomery to support the student sit-ins. In retaliation for a student demonstration at the county courthouse, law officers invaded the campus of Alabama State College with shotguns and threatened to arrest everyone who demonstrated. The young people were further threatened with wholesale expulsion. In this explosive atmosphere, King returned to speak at a student rally. Moreover, he telegraphed an appeal to President Eisenhower, asking "immediate action in your name to restore law and order. . . ." There was no response from Washington.

Meanwhile, sit-ins continued to spread. Realizing that the various independent efforts should be coordinated, King authorized Ella Baker to send out announcements of a youth leadership conference to be held the weekend of April 15-17, 1960. He promised funds from SCLC to help cover expenses. Baker arranged accommodations at Shaw University, the school from which she graduated as valedictorian.

Two hundred students representing at least fifty-six colleges and high schools came to Raleigh, North Carolina that Easter weekend to attend the conference. They found on the campus of the small Southern college a setting of serenity and almost unearthly springtime beauty. Blossoming trees and bushes splashed the grounds with color. Spacious lawns spread a welcoming carpet where the young people could sit and talk.

Ella Baker set the tone in her opening address, "More than a Hamburger." In the deep-throated voice that helped make her a champion debater in college, she urged students to broaden lunch counter desegregation into a movement that would change the whole structure of America. "The younger generation is challenging you and me," she told the adults. "They are asking us to forget our laziness and doubt and fear, and follow our dedication to the truth to the bitter end."

James Lawson received a hero's welcome. The Ph.D. candidate had faced an ultimatum from officials of Vanderbilt University's Divinity School: stop leading sit-ins or leave school. Lawson chose the Freedom Movement and the school expelled him only months before graduation. In his address Lawson charged students to create a climate in the nation to force implementation of legal changes. "Unless we can create the climate, the law can never bring victory," he said. He compared the slow pace of integration in America to the rapid advance of freedom in Africa. "All of Africa," Lawson warned, "will be free before the American Negro attains first-class citizenship."

During the three days, students worked together in groups to share ideas and help solve problems. Adult participants observed; student leaders guided the discussions. The grown-ups were advisors only. All of them agreed with Ella Baker to "speak only when asked to do so."

On Saturday evening King was greeted by a cheering audience assembled in City Auditorium to hear him outline a "Strategy for Victory." His recommendations included expanding the sit-ins into a national campaign of selective buying, boycotting chain stores North and South if any store in the chain practiced segregation. Students cheered loudest when he called for an army of volunteers willing to stay in jail rather than pay fines.

Before the conference ended, the delegates approved the formation of a Temporary Student Nonviolent Coordinating Committee. At later conferences the word "Temporary" was dropped, and the organization became best known by its initials, SNCC, pronounced SNICK. They set as their main goal unequivocal "full equality." For them, litigation (that is, battling in the courts) would be secondary to civil disobedience and mass actions. In their "Statement of Purpose" the students wrote, "We affirm the philosophical or religious ideal of nonviolence. . . . By appealing to conscience and standing on the moral nature of human existence, nonviolence nurtures the atmosphere in which reconciliation and justice become actual possibilities."

Marion Barry from Fisk was elected chairman of the new student group. SNCC decided to remain independent rather than become an affiliate of SCLC or any other existing organization. King gave them temporary office space in a corner of SCLC headquarters in Atlanta.

After the Raleigh conference, Martin King, now thirty-one, hoped for a quiet period to "retreat, concentrate, and reflect." By that spring of 1960, however, he knew that life in Atlanta would be as hectic as it had been in Montgomery. "I must admit," he noted wistfully, "that at times I had felt that I could no longer bear such a heavy burden, and was tempted to retreat to a more quiet and serene life. But every time such a temptation appeared, something came to strengthen and sustain my determination. . . . In the midst of outer dangers I have felt an inner calm."

May brought danger again. The Kings had formed a close friendship with Lillian Smith, the eminent writer. On May 4, after dining together, King and Coretta drove her back to Emory University Hospital where she was undergoing treatment. A police officer stopped the car. In DeKalb County any interracial group was subject to be stopped. Unfortunately, King was driving a borrowed car. Worse, with his busy schedule he had not renewed his driving permit. The ninety-day deadline for doing this had just passed. The officer issued a citation.

When the trial came up, the judge fined King twenty-five dollars and placed him on a year's probation. The probation had far-reaching consequences.

Later that month King returned to Montgomery for the tax fraud trial. He knew the odds against him. "I have been in Alabama courts too many times when the evidence was clearly in my favor, and yet I ended up convicted," he said.

His fate rested with a jury of twelve—all Southerners, all white, all male. Women and blacks could not yet serve on juries in Alabama. For several days King sat in suspense while his interracial team of attorneys presented evidence to prove the charges false. Witnesses who testified on King's behalf included Coretta and King's secretary, Maud Ballou, and Benjamin Mays from Morehouse. King donated part of the royalty from his book, *Stride Toward Freedom,* to Morehouse and to SCLC. The defense attorneys, through skillful cross-examination, tried to show that a portion of the money the tax officials listed as "income" was in fact repayment to King for expenses he incurred during his constant travels.

The case finally went to the jury. Daddy and Mother King, who sat in the courtroom every day, waited with their son in suspense. The prosecution had failed to prove its case of perjury. Still, the accused was a black man, a civil rights leader in the Deep South. After nearly four hours of deliberation, the jury returned to announce the decision. "Not guilty!" For King, the verdict foretold the coming of better race relations in the South.

The sermon King preached the next Sunday at Ebenezer described the past three months of worry over the tax case. His topic was "Autobiography of Suffering." But summer brought happier times. His sister Christine had fallen in love with a young journalist from Missouri, Isaac Newton Harris. Daddy King approved of the "good-looking" fellow who had what he called "a lot of old-fashioned American spine." In August, Christine married Isaac Harris in an elaborate wedding at Ebenezer. Her two brothers performed the ceremonies.

There were happy moments for King and his children, too. He tried to crowd as much time with them as his schedule allowed. Yoki had developed into a plump five-year-old, a photographer's dream in frilly dresses and ribbons. Marty, going on three, loved airplanes because he so often saw his adored father getting on and off them. For the busy father, every moment with his children became a memorable event—reading aloud at bedtime, wrestling together on the floor, watching the glow of a fading sunset, singing together while Coretta played the piano, holding hands and praying before a meal. He did not have to tell his family, "Daddy loves you." They knew it. "It is not the amount but the quality of time that you spend with your children that counts," King said.

There was good news on the political front, too. On May 6, the 1960 Civil Rights Act was signed into law. Although the act was weak, it broadened the powers of the Civil Rights Commission and authorized appointment of referees to help black citizens in their attempts to register and vote.

Another hopeful political signal came from a breakfast meeting on June 22 with the prime contender for the Democratic presidential nomination, John F. Kennedy. King spoke easily with the scholarly, forty-three-year-old Massachusetts senator with curly red hair and a Boston accent. During their ninety-minute talk together, King explained the need for strong presidential leadership in the area of civil rights during the coming months. The next day King wrote, "I was very impressed by the forthright and honest manner in which he discussed the civil rights questions."

In Atlanta, students spent their summer vacation planning a fall sit-in campaign. Store owners had united in solid resistance against the desegregation of eating places. Student leaders, equally determined, decided to pick one target. They chose Rich's, one of the largest department stores in the South. Although most black professionals owned and used Rich's credit cards, they were not allowed to enter the restaurant. "Close out your charge accounts with segregation," students suggested. "Open your account with freedom."

Student leaders scheduled a sit-in at Rich's in October. They wanted wide publicity. The presence of one man could assure that. They went to talk with him.

Martin King faced one more agonizing decision. He felt morally bound to join the students. Yet, he had taken great pains after moving to Atlanta not to upstage any of the established black leaders. His probation, too, on traffic charges stipulated that for twelve months he must not violate any federal or state penal statute.

Three forceful student leaders—Julian Bond, Herchelle Sullivan, and Lonnie King—talked these problems over with their mentor. Martin came to realize how much the Atlanta movement needed him. He agreed to join the students, not as a leader, but as one of the sit-in participants.

On Wednesday, October 19, Richard Rich, the store owner, saw King among the group entering the famed Magnolia Room restaurant. He wept. Personally, he liked King. But he knew his store was in for worldwide publicity. The protesters were arrested, charged with trespassing, and taken to jail. King and the students refused to post bond. That night for the first time in his life King slept in jail.

Hurried meetings among Atlanta's business, political, and civic leaders of both races reached a truce. Late Sunday afternoon the sit-in prisoners left the jail. This was the result of Rich and the state prosecutor agreeing to drop all charges. All, that is, except King. Authorities in DeKalb County,

Georgia insisted that he had violated his probation and demanded custody over him.

Reverend A. D. King watched in consternation as his brother was handcuffed and placed in a DeKalb sheriff's car. A huge German shepherd dog guarded him on the back seat.

The next Tuesday, Daddy King, Christine and A. D. came to the hearing in the DeKalb County Courthouse. The testimony from King, and from distinguished Atlanta citizens, had no effect upon the final outcome. Judge J. Oscar Mitchell read the verdict: "I find the defendant guilty, and sentence him to six months in the State Penitentiary at Reidsville." King's lawyers asked that the prisoner be released on bond pending appeal. Judge Mitchell denied the motion.

Never before had Coretta lost her composure in public, but the thought of what might happen to her husband in the notorious Reidsville prison caused her to break down in tears.

"Corrie, dear, you have to be strong," her husband consoled her. "You have to be strong for me."

Daddy King reassured them in his own style. "I am ready to fight. When you see Daddy crying, Coretta, then you start crying."

King was returned to his jail cell. In the pre-dawn darkness the next morning he awoke suddenly as jailers played a flashlight over his face. "Get up, King—Did you hear me, King?" One of them ordered, "Get up and come on out here, and bring all your things with you."

Shackled in handcuffs and leg irons, King was shoved in the back seat of a car, while two deputies sat up front. They refused to tell King where they were going. For two hours they drove through the dark countryside. From boyhood he had heard stories of black prisoners listed as "escapees" who suddenly disappeared and were never heard of again. When daylight came he realized they were headed for Reidsville.

In Reidsville, the minister and civil rights leader was treated the same as common criminals and was forced to dress in the striped prison garb.

From his cell he wrote to comfort his wife: ". . . this is the cross we must bear for the freedom of our people." He pleaded with Coretta not to worry about him, reassuring her, "I will adjust to whatever comes in terms of pain."

King's jailing in Reidsville brought speedy reactions on the national and international scene. One morning Coretta answered her phone and heard a familiar Boston accent.

"Good morning, Mrs. King. This is Senator Kennedy."

For a few minutes the two exchanged pleasantries. Then Senator Kennedy said, "I want to express to you my concern about your husband. I know this must be very hard on you. I understand you are expecting a baby, and I just wanted you to know that I was thinking about you and Dr. King." Before hanging up, he added, "If there is anything I can do to help, please feel free to call on me."

Meanwhile, John Kennedy's brother and campaign manager, Robert Kennedy, telephoned Judge Mitchell. Did King not have a constitutional right to bail for such a minor offense? he questioned. Judge Mitchell was forced to agree that, indeed, King had that right. Under pressure, he granted King's release on bail. The Republican presidential candidate, Richard Nixon, by contrast, elected to remain silent.

King's return from Reidsville illustrated how quickly events for him and the civil rights movement could shift from one day to another. A plane chartered by SCLC and a limousine transported him home for a welcoming celebration at Ebenezer. As the car crossed into Fulton County, one hundred students lined up to form an honor guard. Pat Watters, a reporter, scrawled notes in his journal that give a memorable picture of the scene.

"He was younger looking than I expected. . . . A look of vulnerability about him—not softness, not naiveté, but somehow hurtable." The reporter recorded the students' welcome. "Dr. King got out of his car and waved to them; they began to sing. . . . I stood there listening in the moonlight, a soft wind breathing. . . . They were so young, so unafraid."

At Ebenezer King spoke about his prison life, and talked of his gratitude to the Kennedy brothers. He was president of SCLC, which politically was a non-partisan organization. He decided that he would not publicly endorse Kennedy as the Democratic Party's candidate for president.

Daddy King, on the other hand, felt free to speak his mind. A staunch Republican, he now experienced a change of heart. "Take off your Nixon buttons!" he told his congregation. His son safe, he cried out: "If I had a suitcase full of votes, I'd dump as many of them as I could right in John Kennedy's lap!" Kennedy's victory in the 1960 elections, indeed, was attributed in no small part to the heavy black vote that he had won.

In this fashion the sixties began. In that single year, 1960, more than fifty thousand people took to the streets to protest racial segregation. In city after city, stores either changed their policies or went out of business thanks to sit-ins, boycotts, and picketing.

Before 1960 black Americans were struggling for integration—to have the right to join the American mainstream, to belong. The students changed the struggle, and raised it to a new level. What had begun as a bus boycott in Montgomery was becoming a revolution to win for black people the inalienable rights promised in 1776 and 1863 but never fully achieved. "Freedom!" was now the rallying cry.

6

THE FREEDOM RIDE, 1961-1962

A piece of freedom is no longer
enough for human beings. . . .
Freedom is like life. It cannot be had
in installments.

MLK

The year 1961 began happily for Coretta and Martin King. On January 30, their second son was born. They named him Dexter Scott, to honor the Montgomery church and Coretta's family.

In April, King went to Washington to see Attorney General Robert Kennedy. The two, who had become friends, talked about harassment of black riders who sat on front seats of trains and buses in the Deep South. A 1946 Supreme Court case had banned forced segregation on vehicles in interstate travel. Another case in 1960 brought an end to segregated waiting rooms, restrooms, and eating places. Yet, blacks who tried to exercise their constitutional rights in these areas were beaten and often thrown off trains and buses.

King urged Kennedy to enforce the Supreme Court mandates. The Interstate Commerce Commission (ICC), which governed interstate travel, was under the Justice Department.

Later that month, James Farmer, the new executive director of the Congress of Racial Equality (CORE), telephoned King about the same matter. Farmer, a trained minister, had helped to organize CORE in 1942. It was a Chicago group of young people who experimented in using nonviolent direct action to challenge racial discrimination.

Farmer talked to King that April 1961 about his plans for "putting the movement on wheels." The Freedom Ride, as he called the project, would be patterned after a 1947 test trip called a "Journey of Reconciliation," which was sponsored by CORE and the Fellowship of Reconciliation. The journey took an interracial group by bus and train through the Upper South—Kentucky, Tennessee, North Carolina, and Virginia. Publicizing the Supreme Court ruling of 1946 it urged blacks to sit where they pleased during interstate travel. The 1947 journey did not receive much publicity: in the Upper South there was little violence.

Farmer, in 1961, followed the Ghandian principle of informing governmental leaders about his plans. He sent letters to President Kennedy, to the FBI, the ICC, and to the heads of the bus companies that were to be involved. He included maps to show how the Freedom Ride would take a zigzag route through Virginia and the Carolinas, across Georgia, Alabama, and Mississippi, then down to Louisiana. It would culminate in a rally in New Orleans on May 17, to commemorate the seventh anniversary of the *Brown* school desegregation decision.

James Farmer knew that an interracial group in the Deep South would invite confrontation. This would attract news reporters and generate publicity. Then, he thought, the executive and judicial branches of the federal government would be compelled by public outrage to take action. James Farmer was frank about his objective: "to prod the Department of Justice into enforcing the law of the land."

Farmer gave a copy of the Freedom Ride itinerary to his father, who was hospitalized with terminal cancer. James Farmer, Sr., a minister and scholar educated at Boston University, could read, write, and speak Hebrew, Greek, Latin, French, and German. He had become widely known, as professor or dean, at a number of black colleges. When Dr. Farmer learned of his son's mission, tears welled in his eyes. "Son," he said, "I wish you wouldn't go. But at the same time, I am more proud than I have ever been in my life because you are going. Please try to survive."

Martin King gave full support to CORE's protest movement. He promised that SCLC chapters would be informed and urged each to welcome and help the riders at the stops along the way. Later he served on the Freedom Ride Coordinating Committee.

Applicants for the Freedom Ride were screened; sixteen were chosen. Their ages ranged from eighteen years to sixty-one. One of them was James Peck, son of the owners of New York's Peck and Peck, women's clothiers. Another participant was John Lewis, veteran of the Nashville sit-ins. "At this time," Lewis said when he volunteered, "human dignity is the most important thing in my life."

In addition to Lewis and Peck, the volunteers chosen included Dr. Walter Bergman, a professor at the University of Michigan, and his wife, Frances; Reverend B. Elton Cox, a black minister; Albert Bigelow, a former Navy captain; Hank Thomas, a Howard University senior and sit-in veteran; Ed Blankenheim, a CORE activist; Charles Person, who was jailed during the Atlanta sit-ins; and Genevieve Hughes, Jimmy McDonald, and Joe Perkins, who were CORE staff members.

These volunteers came to Washington at the end of April 1961 for intensive training. James Farmer explained the purpose of the project. A lawyer gave a briefing on their legal rights and what they should do if arrested. A social scientist explained the folkways of the Deep South. A social activist indicated frankly what might happen, including beatings and even death. The discussions were followed by role-playing sessions. Some played the part of Freedom Riders while others pretended to be racists who challenged them. Group members then reversed roles to get a feel for both sides. They "practiced" being knocked off lunch-counter stools, stomped, kicked, and subjected to every possible kind of harassment. "Realism was imperative," Farmer wrote later, "so that we could learn how to reduce the probability of serious and permanent damage in the real-life situation facing us."

ROUTE OF 'FREEDOM RIDERS' *

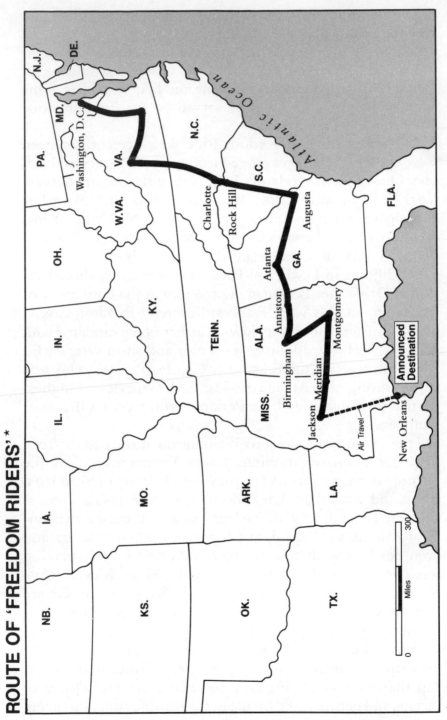

* 1" = 200 miles.

On the evening of May 3, each volunteer was given the op-
tion to quit if he or she had doubts about the project. CORE
would pay transportation back home. But next morning,
every volunteer showed up at the bus terminal.

The group split up into interracial teams, half of them
boarding Trailways, and the other half Greyhound. The buses
rolled down the highways. A new phase in the Freedom
Movement began.

In Virginia and North Carolina, many of the Jim Crow
signs came down before the Freedom Riders arrived. The first
serious problem with racists came in Rock Hill, South
Carolina. John Lewis walked toward the waiting room
labeled "For Whites." Two tough-looking white youths in
leather jackets stopped him. "Get to the other side where
niggers go," they ordered Lewis.

"I have a right to go in there," Lewis answered in his usual
dignified manner. He even quoted the Supreme Court case
that gave the constitutional right to use any waiting room in
interstate terminals. As he tried to pass the toughs they
knocked him to the floor and began to stomp him. Albert
Bigelow, the Navy captain, stepped between Lewis and his
attackers. Only then did a policeman, who had watched it all,
come to chase the toughs away. Both Lewis and Bigelow
followed their training in nonviolent resistance. As James
Farmer wrote, "Thanks to Martin Luther King, Jr., and the
sit-in movement that had roared across the South,
nonviolence was now a popular concept."

The Freedom Ride continued, with John Lewis wearing
Band-Aids to cover cuts over his eyebrow. There were happy
times along the way to balance the unpleasant encounters. At
every overnight stop, the black community staged rallies to
show appreciation. Whether in a church or on a college
campus, each Freedom Rider was introduced, and received
applause befitting a celebrity.

James Farmer called King to give the time of their arrival in
Atlanta, where the riders would spend two nights and a full
day, sleeping in the dormitories of Atlanta University. King
invited the entire group to have dinner with him at a black-

owned restaurant. He listened intently as one rider after another gave details about the trip. Their Freedom Ride, he told them, demonstrated nonviolent direct action at its best. He was proud, he said, to be a member of the CORE National Advisory Board.

When the group left Georgia and headed into Alabama, they knew that they were facing the most dangerous leg of their journey. Farmer announced that during the ride through Alabama he would be in charge in one bus, and James Peck in the other.

Up to that point, the elder Farmer had clung to life; every day, from his bed in Washington's Freedmen's Hospital, he followed the map his son had given him. "Well, let's see where Junior is today," he would say. The night before James Farmer was scheduled to go into Alabama, Dr. Farmer died. Farmer had to leave to bury his father. The other riders went on without him.

On May 14 the Greyhound bus pulled into the terminal at Anniston. When they left, a mob of angry whites armed with an assortment of lethal weapons followed them in cars. Hank Thomas watched and reported later, "They shot the tires out. . . . And we were trapped on the bus. . . . first they closed the doors and wouldn't let us off." The bus was burning and those inside remembered that the driver had recently filled the gas tank. Someone yelled out, "Hey, the bus is gonna explode." The mob scattered. Then Albert Bigelow, the former Navy commander schooled in giving orders under fire, coolly got the emergency door open and evacuated the passengers quickly. Minutes later the bus exploded and burned to a charred frame. Even as Hank Thomas ran from the flames he "got whacked over the head with a rod. . . ." Other riders were beaten by the mob or cut by shattered glass from the exploding bus. When they were taken to a hospital for medical treatment, Thomas reported, "The people at the hospital wouldn't do anything for us."

Reverend Fred Shuttlesworth of Birmingham, Alabama saved them. As head of the SCLC affiliate in Birmingham, he had planned to welcome the Freedom Riders when they reached his city. The young minister had met with King at least once each month during the Montgomery bus boycott, and later he started a similar movement in Birmingham. One of the SCLC founders, he became secretary when King was elected president. He was known as a lion-hearted minister who never shrank from facing racists head-on, even after his house had been bombed and his life threatened.

When Shuttlesworth heard reports of the violence at Anniston, he immediately made an announcement over the radio: "I'm going to get my people. I'm a nonviolent man, but I'm going to get my people." Other black leaders joined his fifteen-car caravan that went along the road with shotguns sticking out of the windows. Nobody interfered, neither the Klan nor the police; they knew that Shuttlesworth meant business. He rescued the Freedom Riders and took them to Birmingham.

Meanwhile, when the Trailways bus crossed the Alabama state line, a half dozen white toughs came aboard, brandishing brass knuckles, blackjacks, pieces of chains, and pistols. Beating the riders they forced them to the back of the bus. Dr. Bergman came to the aid of the victims, but was knocked down and kicked in the head. "They used my husband's head like a football," Frances Bergman said. Later he suffered a cerebral hemorrhage as a result of these blows. The blood-spattered bus continued on to Birmingham. "It looks like there's been a hog-killing on this bus," one of the passengers exclaimed.

The Trailways bus pulled into the Birmingham bus terminal on May 14, Mother's Day. From the windows the riders could see gangs of white men with chains and baseball bats, but not a police officer in sight. "Police did not arrive until ten minutes later," wrote a CBS reporter, "when the hoodlums got into waiting cars and moved down the street."

James Peck, in charge of the bus, looked at Pearson, one of the riders. Pearson said, "Let's go." "As we entered the white waiting room and approached the lunch counter," wrote Peck later, "we were grabbed bodily and pushed toward the alleyway. . . . Six of them started swinging at me with fists and pipes. Five others attacked Pearson . . . . Within seconds I was unconscious." Peck was taken to a hospital; his wounds needed fifty-three stitches to close. Other riders met similar treatment.

When Fred Shuttlesworth and two members of his church finally drove the battered Freedom Riders back to the bus station, Greyhound and Trailway buses had had enough; the drivers refused to take them any further. Next day the riders decided to board a flight to New Orleans in order to arrive in time for the May 17 celebration. A mob gathered at the airport before they took off to continue the beatings of the day before. Police finally cleared the airport so that the group might embark upon an Eastern Airlines plane.

Thus the first chapter of the Freedom Ride came to a close. Unlike the 1947 journey, it generated worldwide publicity. Pictures of the charred Greyhound bus, of James Peck with his head and face swathed in bandages, circulated around the globe. Messages came from friends in Japan, Poland, South Africa. The world was watching; Washington knew it.

News of the beatings not only roused the world, but also the entire civil rights movement. When sit-in veterans saw what had happened in Alabama, they at once took action. The young people felt a commitment to carry on the protest. John Lewis had left the group temporarily to keep an appointment for a crucial interview, so he missed the Alabama trip. He met with Diane Nash and other leaders of the Nashville Student Movement. If the Freedom Ride did not go on, they decided, segregationists might believe that intimidation could stop future civil rights demonstrations.

Diane Nash telephoned James Farmer. "Would you have any objection to members of the Nashville Student Movement, which is SNCC, going in and taking up where CORE left off?"

"You realize it might be suicidal?" Farmer asked.

"We fully realize that, but we cannot let them stop us with violence. If we do, the movement is dead."

John Lewis and nine other sit-in veterans bought tickets for Birmingham. The Freedom Ride continued. "These people faced the probability of their own death before they left Nashville," Diane said later. "Several made out wills. A few gave me sealed letters to be mailed if they were killed."

The trip went well until the bus reached the Birmingham station. There, the police took command, and taped newspaper over all the bus windows. The Freedom Riders had no way of knowing what would happen to them. Nobody could see inside and they could not see what was taking place outside. Into the tense situation stepped a man they would come to know well in future weeks—Birmingham's police chief Eugene Connor, nicknamed "Bull." Sixty-three years of age, stout, and with greying hair, Connor looked at the group. He ordered the students arrested and placed under police custody.

Connor was dealing with a new breed of blacks. John Lewis reported later what happened that Wednesday night. "We didn't eat anything. We went on a hunger strike." Thursday, the young people stayed in jail, still refusing to eat. Around midnight, Bull Connor came into the jail and spoke to the Freedom Riders. "We are taking you back to Nashville, back to the college campus where you belong," he told them.

"We plan to go to Montgomery, and from Montgomery we're going to New Orleans," the group answered back. They then went limp and refused to move. Connor's officers picked the students up bodily, placed them in cars, and drove them to the Alabama-Tennessee border. Lewis rode with Connor and saw another side of the chief's personality. Connor talked and joked with the students, and even promised to join them for breakfast one day after they went back to school.

Bull Connor left the students on the highway at night, with strict instructions to take a bus back to Tennessee. Instead, the determined young people walked on in the darkness, located a black family, and telephoned Diane Nash to send cars. Diane gave them the good news that more volunteers were on the way.

Meanwhile, Washington reacted. Attorney General Robert Kennedy heated-up the lines to Alabama officials and started behind-the-scenes negotiations. As for the President, he wanted the protest stopped. "Tell them to call it off!" he ordered. The publicity over the Freedom Riders came at a time when John Kennedy was preparing for a summit conference with Soviet Premier Nikita Khrushchev. The bad publicity was embarrassing for the United States. Robert Kennedy, after much discussion, finally persuaded Alabama Governor John Patterson to send state police to escort the Freedom Riders into Montgomery. Kennedy also sent his deputy, Byron White, and his public affairs assistant, John Siegenthaler, a journalist, to talk with local officials.

Twenty-one new Freedom Riders left Birmingham on May 20. A private airplane flew overhead to spot trouble. State patrol cars were stationed every few miles along the highway. Everything seemed peaceful. The riders relaxed. When they reached the outskirts of Montgomery, however, all protection disappeared without warning.

John Lewis described their arrival. "That bus station had become a ghost town, that whole area. It was an eerie feeling. . . . Complete silence. . . . We stepped off the bus and . . . people started pouring out of the station, out of buildings, from all over the place. White people . . . ."

James Swerg, a student from Fisk, got off the bus. The sight of the handsome young white man dressed in an olive green business suit aroused the fury of the mob. "Kill the nigger-loving sonofabitch," a woman screamed. The toughs pounded Swerg with bats until he fell; they pushed his face into the hot tar of the roadway.

Ruby Doris Smith, a Spelman student, described the beatings. "The mob turned from Swerg to us. . . . I saw John Lewis beaten, blood coming out of his mouth." Lewis' suitcase was ripped apart, scattering clothes and mail. The crowd gathered up his belongings and made a bonfire.

John Siegenthaler tried to get some of the young women into his car. He was struck from behind with a pipe and knocked senseless. Robert Kennedy's assistant lay unconscious for a full hour before anybody sent for help. John Doar, a high official in the Department of Justice's Civil Rights

Division, put through a call to the attorney general. "It's terrible," he told Kennedy, "there's not a cop in sight. . . ."

Many of the Freedom Riders were badly hurt; miraculously, none was killed. Members of the Montgomery Improvement Association took them, bleeding and bandaged, into their homes, and gave them shelter. MIA people knew only too well what racial hatred meant, the spiritual as well as physical agonies that racial violence inflicts upon its victims. They had lived through it all during the bus boycott.

The president and the attorney general were now obliged to act. John Kennedy, for sure, did not wish to offend powerful Southern politicians who had helped put him in office, but the public outcry gave him no alternative. The attorney general announced that the Department of Justice would take action against the Klan and any other group that was disrupting interstate travel. He would seek, he said, a court order, or injunction, to prohibit such interference. He mobilized federal marshals, and ordered them into Montgomery. He persuaded the governor of Alabama to call up the National Guard.

Martin King and Ralph Abernathy learned of events in Montgomery while they were in Chicago for a speaking engagement. At once they boarded a plane. Late on Saturday night they met with the Freedom Riders in Montgomery and planned a rally at the First Baptist Church, to be held on Sunday night. It was scheduled to start at eight o'clock.

At six o'clock on Sunday night the church was already jammed. News that the Freedom Riders would be there had brought racist groups into town from all over the surrounding countryside. Bobby Kennedy stayed by his phone, and kept in close touch with the situation.

Federal marshals formed a ring around Martin King and brought him safely into the church. Freedom Riders were in the choir stand, disguised as members of the choir. John Lewis wore a cap to hide the patch on his head.

Shuttlesworth was not there: He had driven to the airport to pick up James Farmer. As he and Farmer neared the church they saw hundreds of whites standing guard with clubs. The situation did not phase the lion-hearted Shuttlesworth. Striding through the crowd like he was a commanding general, he barked "Out of the way. Go on. Out of the way!" Farmer followed him into the building before the mobsters, dazed by such bravado, could react.

Darkness deepened. The crowd outside grew to several thousand. The sound of prayers and freedom songs could be heard from within; the mob's mood turned savage. Rocks smashed through the stained-glass windows, shattering the panes, scattering slivers and splinters everywhere within. Voices were screaming taunts, threats to burn the building to the ground.

King spoke to the people, urging them to keep their courage high at this terrifying moment. "We are going to continue to stand for what is right," he said. "The main thing I want to say to you is fear not, we've come too far to turn back. . . ." When it seemed as if the mob were at the point of breaking in, he said: "Let us join hands together and sing."

Bobby Kennedy, now seriously worried, got on the phone to Governor Patterson of Alabama and asked him to have the National Guard move into the church area at once to reinforce the marshals.

The governor answered that the commander of the Guard would not be able to guarantee Martin King's safety. "Have the general call me," Kennedy snapped, "I want him to say it to me. I want to hear a general of the U.S. Army say he can't protect Martin Luther King, Jr."

That was enough for Governor Patterson. He declared martial law and sealed off the church. State police and the National Guard moved in to disperse the crowd. As dawn broke on Monday morning, officers escorted the churchgoers, exhausted by the all-night ordeal, to their homes.

The students were now more determined than ever to continue the Freedom Ride. By Monday new volunteers, most of them students, joined the protest. On Tuesday, King, Farmer, Abernathy, Nash, and Lewis sat together at a press conference. The Freedom Ride would continue, they announced. The first buses would leave the next day for Mississippi.

A disappointing moment came for the students when they learned King was not going with them. It was another painful choice Martin King had to make. He was conscious that he had become a symbol, and his going would inspire others. On the other hand, he needed to be free to raise funds and help direct the course of rapidly-moving events. Many SNCC members never forgave him for not getting on that bus to Mississippi.

Armed National Guardsmen escorted the Freedom Riders to the bus station as they boarded two buses, both heavily guarded, for Jackson, Mississippi. Three airplanes and two helicopters flew overhead. Other armed units patrolled the highway. At one point Farmer, who also had been reluctant to join the group, saw students writing on slips of paper. "They were writing the names and addresses of their next of kin," he wrote later. Facing a nonviolent struggle, they prepared themselves for it like soldiers going into battle. Soon they began to sing a song that raised their spirits. The verses had been specially composed for this occasion. The song itself, "Hallelujah, I'm A-Travelin'," was a parody of a song that had been popular during the Depression. Some of the young people on the Freedom Ride may well have learned it from their parents.

At the Mississippi state line, patrolmen took over protection of the two buses. This was the deal made between Robert Kennedy and Mississippi senator James Eastland. As soon as students tried to integrate facilities they would be arrested. Kennedy reasoned that students would accept bail, take a return bus home, and that would end the crisis.

All twenty-seven were arrested that first day. Trial and sentencing were cut and dried: Sixty days' suspended sentence and a fine of two hundred dollars. The riders refused to pay the fine, which they considered unconstitutional. All elected to keep their "jail-no-bail" vow.

Attorney General Kennedy telephoned Martin King, promising to use his powers and get the arrested students out of jail. King gave the attorney general a lesson on civil disobedience. "Our conscience tells us that the law is wrong and

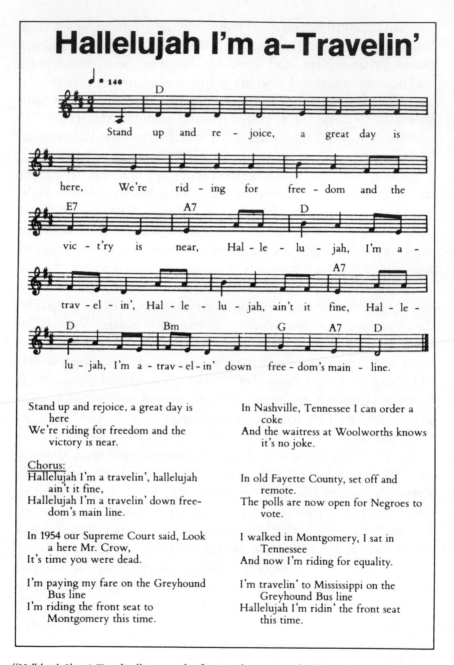

Hallelujah I'm a-Travelin'

Stand up and rejoice, a great day is
here
We're riding for freedom and the
victory is near.

Chorus:
Hallelujah I'm a travelin', hallelujah
ain't it fine,
Hallelujah I'm a travelin' down freedom's main line.

In 1954 our Supreme Court said, Look
a here Mr. Crow,
It's time you were dead.

I'm paying my fare on the Greyhound
Bus line
I'm riding the front seat to
Montgomery this time.

In Nashville, Tennessee I can order a
coke
And the waitress at Woolworths knows
it's no joke.

In old Fayette County, set off and
remote.
The polls are now open for Negroes to
vote.

I walked in Montgomery, I sat in
Tennessee
And now I'm riding for equality.

I'm travelin' to Mississippi on the
Greyhound Bus line
Hallelujah I'm ridin' the front seat
this time.

"Hallelujah I'm A-Traveling" is a parody of a song that was popular during the Great Depression, "Hallelujah I'm a Bum." Some of the young people on the Freedom Ride may well have learned it from their parents.

we must resist," King said, "but we have a moral obligation to accept the penalty." He thanked Kennedy, and added, "I see a ray of hope, but I am different than my father. I feel the need of being free now."

"If they want to get out, we can get them out," Kennedy insisted.

"They'll stay." King felt a close kinship with the uncompromising Freedom Riders. At one of their training sessions he had encouraged them to "develop the quiet courage of dying for a cause." The riders had the courage. These young people, who had left behind the security of college campuses and comfortable homes, stayed in their jail cells.

One day a black trustee who had the run of the jail whispered a warning to Farmer. "They're gonna send you to the prison farm. That's where they're gonna break you. . . ." The trustee was right. The Freedom Riders were later sent to the state prison at Parchman. They talked later about the dehumanizing conditions that they found there. The cells were damp, and cold at night. Lying on their bug-infested mattresses, the Freedom Riders sang together to keep their spirits high. The singing infuriated the white guards because the songs were mostly of freedom. "If you don't stop singing, we'll take away your mattresses," guards warned. James Farmer told how guards yanked their mattresses off the beds, leaving the singers on the cold, hard metal frames. Guards sometimes opened windows and turned on exhaust fans to bring in the cold night air.

One of the fearsome punishments for "uppity" students was the use of electric cattle prods. Cordell Reagon remembered the horror of seeing them applied to two pacifists who refused to strip off their clothing. "So they used cattle-prodders on them," he related. "They put the cattle prods up and down their bodies . . . about thirty times—which left black marks all over their bodies."

Stokely Carmichael, a student from Howard University, had excelled in the Bronx High School of Science, reserved for top New York City students. He loved to sing and tease tough Sheriff Tyson. Stokely told how one day Tyson tried to take his mattress. "I hung on to the mattress. . . . I wouldn't move and I started to sing 'I'm Gonna Tell God How You Treat Me,' and everybody started to sing it; and by this time Tyson was really to pieces. . . ."

Jailed riders told stories of hard work in the fields from dawn til dusk, glass found in the food, heads pounded against concrete blocks, cries and moans of friends being beaten. These stories of horror did not stem the flow of student volunteers who came South to fill the Mississippi jails. They came from all races, all faiths, all sections of the country. The Freedom Ride had become, for them, a crusade. College classes, family loyalties, material comforts, good times, all were willingly abandoned as the Freedom Movement, with its irresistible call, drew them to itself. Many of these young people, too, did not just leave home for a brief time. They made plans to stay in the Deep South and to work among the black people who lived there.

Martin King tried to explain their attitude to an uncomprehending adult society. These students were "carrying forward a revolutionary destiny of a whole people, consciously and deliberately," he wrote in the *New York Times Magazine*. "Hence the extraordinary willingness to fill the jails as if they were honor classes."

The Freedom Ride brought the results James Farmer had anticipated. Attorney General Robert Kennedy directed the Interstate Commerce Commission to issue a regulation banning all segregation in interstate travel facilities, effective November 1, 1961. Eventually, Jim Crow signs in terminals would become mere historic artifacts. "A remarkable victory," King called the ruling.

The victory for black Americans extended far beyond visible changes seen on trains and buses, in dining areas, and restrooms. The psychological triumph began to heal deep scars that had shackled the race for centuries. Segregation stood as a badge of slavery, signifying that blacks could never be equal to whites. The Montgomery protest, the sit-ins, and the Freedom Rides combined to neutralize insecurities, and to give Southern blacks a sense of their power and their role in American history.

Courage became contagious. By the close of 1961, it was fashionable to be part of the Freedom Movement. One minister noted, "Once I thought it was a disgrace to get involved. Now it's a disgrace not to be involved." A black woman put it differently. "It's like a fever. It's catching."

The fever also affected established civil rights organizations, all competing for membership and funds. The young people had seized the initiative and the publicity. Their leaders were forced to appraise their traditional, patient approaches. They stepped-up timetables for achieving full equality.

Perhaps the greatest impact of the Freedom Ride was upon the young people who took part. Cordell Reagon summed it up when he said, "So that's when I got . . . really involved in the movement. That's when I stopped thinking it was just something exciting."

The punishment suffered in Parchman broke some of the riders, physically and mentally; it strengthened others emotionally. Many emerged from the experience hardened and changed. Brilliant young students entered the Mississippi prison with faith in Gandhi's *satyagraha,* love force, to win over white Americans. They left with the belief that one force, and one alone, would dictate change: power! And this power would come to blacks through voting strength. Many Freedom Riders decided to stay in Mississippi. SNCC launched a two-pronged program, with some workers continuing direct-action demonstrations, while others became field workers, living and working among poor, voiceless blacks, opening Freedom Schools, developing voter-education projects.

Dr. Martin Luther King, Jr. took stock of his own leadership. Since his return from India his life had been directed largely by events, requests, emergencies. It was time for him to seize the initiative. Young black activists were beginning to question his leadership ability, thinking him too slow, too patient, too accommodating with Washington officials.

He continued to strengthen SCLC as an operating base. Reverend Wyatt Tee Walker, six-foot and energetic, had taken over as executive director of SCLC. Ella Baker had worked miracles with her staff of one secretary, but she was not a minister, and she was a woman. In the minister-dominated SCLC, she was never given the full authority she needed to build the organization. Also, she often clashed with King over the direction SCLC should follow, and felt the organization was dominated too much by the strong personality of its president.

From behind his horn-rimmed glasses Walker surveyed the situation and began to make improvements. He launched fund-raising drives and increased the SCLC treasury. This meant money to hire a larger staff, to encourage formation of new affiliates, and to develop new projects. Walker influenced a former schoolmate, Walter Fauntroy, pastor of a Washington church, to head an SCLC bureau in the nation's capital. A Western Christian Leadership Conference was formed in California.

Another promising young minister who joined the SCLC staff during the summer of 1961 was Andrew Young. Son of a prosperous New Orleans dentist, Young was schooled at Howard University and Hartford Theological Seminary. He was ordained as a Congregational minister and from 1957 to 1961 served as one of only three black executives in the National Council of Churches.

Andrew Young set to work to organize SCLC's Voter Education Project. The purpose of this project was to train volunteers who would launch voter-registration campaigns in their hometowns explaining the importance of voting and teaching people how to do it. Assisting him were Dorothy Cotton and Septima Poinsette Clark, remarkable black women with a genius for teaching the poor and the non-literate.   The centennial of the Emancipation Proclamation, 1963, was drawing near. Martin King now made his plans to continue the freedom struggle.

7

ALBANY AND BIRMINGHAM, 1961-1963

> To suffer in a righteous cause is to grow to our humanity's full stature. If only to save ourselves, we need the vision to see the ordeals of this generation as the opportunity to transform ourselves and American society.
>
> MLK

"WE URGE YOU TO COME AND JOIN THE ALBANY MOVEMENT." The telegraphed plea from a Morehouse schoolmate brought King into the Albany protest. His long-time friend, William Anderson, had become a doctor and now headed a group of organizations called "The Albany Movement."

Albany had once been a slave-trading center for southwest Georgia. In 1961, blacks had no power in running the city. White leaders refused to even talk with black leaders about making changes.

The night King came to speak at a rally, black citizens let him know how they felt. "Martin Luther King says free-dom!" they shouted. "Let the white man say free-dom." Caught up in the fervor, King told them, "We will win with the power of our capacity to endure." And the crowd shouted back, "Hallelujah!"

Albany's protesters, largely students, were already schooled in nonviolent techniques. Two Freedom Riders,

Keep On a-Walkin'

Ain't gonna let no - bod - y, Law - dy,
turn me 'round, turn me 'round, turn me 'round.
Ain't gon - na let no - bod - y, Law - dy,
turn me 'round; Keep on a - walk - in', (yea!)
Keep on a - talk - in', (yea!)
March - in' on to Free - dom land.

Ain't gonna let segregation, Lawdy, turn me 'round, turn me
'round, turn me 'round
Ain't gonna let segregation, Lawdy, turn me 'round,
Keep on a-walkin', (yea!)
Keep on a-talkin', (yea!)
Marchin' on to Freedom land.

Ain't gonna let no jailhouse, Lawdy, turn me 'round, turn me
                        'round, turn me 'round,
Ain't gonna let no jailhouse, Lawdy, turn me 'round,
    Keep on a-walkin', (yea!)
    Keep on a-talkin', (yea!)
Marchin' on to Freedom land.

Ain't gonna let no nervous Nelly, Lawdy, turn me 'round,
                  turn me 'round, turn me 'round,
Ain't gonna let no nervous Nelly, Lawdy, turn me 'round,
    Keep on a-walkin', (yea!)
    Keep on a-talkin', (yea!)
Marchin' on to Freedom land.

Ain't gonna let Chief Pritchett, turn me 'round, turn me 'round,
                              turn me 'round,
Ain't gonna let Chief Pritchett, turn me 'round,
    Keep on a-walkin', (yea!)
    Keep on a-talkin', (yea!)
Marchin' on to Freedom land.

Ain't gonna let no shotgun, turn me 'round, turn me 'round,
                        turn me 'round,
Ain't gonna let no shotgun, turn me 'round,
    Keep on a-walkin', (yca!)
    Keep on a-talkin', (yea!)
Marchin' on to Freedom land.

Ain't gonna let no Uncle Tom, Lawdy, turn me 'round, turn
                     me 'round, turn me 'round.
Ain't gonna let no Uncle Tom, Lawdy, turn me 'round,
    Keep on a-walkin', (yea!)
    Keep on a-talkin', (yea!)
Marchin' on to Freedom land.

Ain't gonna let nobody, etc.

This song, sung to the tune of an old spiritual, was born out of the demonstrations that took place in Albany, Georgia, in July 1962. It has since become one of the most popular of all the modern freedom songs. It was sung by thousands at the March on Washington of August 1963. (Source: The Ballad of America by John A. Scott. Used by permission.)

Cordell Reagon, eighteen, and Charles Sherrod, twenty-two, came to Albany after they left Parchman prison. They set up workshops to teach nonviolent direct action. The NAACP Youth Council at all-black Albany State College began a series of sit-ins and marches to publicize the rigid segregation that prevailed in Albany.

This movement failed to grow. Chief of Police Laurie Pritchett was a shrewd antagonist. He developed his own techniques to suppress the agitation while at the same time avoiding publicity. Demonstrators were arrested and then dispersed to jails in nearby counties; there was no concentration of victims to be the subject of press pictures and to arouse public awareness of the struggle and sympathy for it.

Martin King, too, was arrested three times after he came to Albany. Each time Pritchett turned him loose again before hundreds of sympathizers, pouring into town, could bring with them news publicity and television coverage.

The Albany Movement, therefore, did not succeed in generating enough pressure upon the city's leaders to bring them to the negotiating table. Many critics accepted the verdict of a Northern newspaper, that Albany "was one of the most stunning defeats of Martin King's career."

King turned the Albany experience to good advantage as a lesson from which he could learn how to conduct a freedom struggle. Goals, he realized, must be few, and clearly defined. Negotiated agreements must be in writing. The black community must be united behind the movement; its leader must be recognized by all; there must be no factional quarreling. Next time, he resolved, the target city would be of his own choosing.

He selected Birmingham, Alabama, the "biggest, toughest, most segregated city in the South." It was a great steel- and iron-producing center where segregation was rigidly and brutally enforced. Reverend Fred Shuttlesworth had been carrying on a struggle there to integrate public facilities ever since the Montgomery bus boycott. The white response was: *never*. If the movement won a victory at Birmingham, King believed, it would affect the course of the struggle in cities all over the South.

Late in 1962 SCLC staff and legal advisors laid their plans. The Birmingham project was given the code name C—for Confrontation. It was launched on Wednesday April 3, 1963, later than had originally been planned. The delay gave King a chance to go back to Atlanta to check on Coretta, who was expecting the birth of their fourth child. "Martin was there," she said, "to take me to the hospital, but the next day, after the baby was born, he left for Birmingham. Then he dashed back to Atlanta in time to bring me home." The baby was named Bernice Albertine (Bunny for short) for her two grand-mothers.

Project C was conducted in separate phases, with a series of struggles building toward a climax. James Bevel described it when he said, "Every nonviolent movement is a dialogue." The main goals of Project C were desegregation of public facilities in downtown department stores, fair hiring practices in business and government, and the establishment of a bira-cial committee to explore ways of improving race relations.

Phase one of Project C was launched with a printed *Birmingham Manifesto* to call the black community to action. "The patience of an oppressed people cannot endure forever," it said; "our protest is the sole meaningful alternative. . . . We act in full concert with the law of morality and the Constitu-tion of our nation. . . ." Small groups picketed department stores or held sit-ins at lunch counters. Each day brought predictable arrests, but the demonstrators were not many. Tension was to build slowly.

As in Montgomery the black churches served as a central force for the organization, mobilization, and direction of the protest. The rallies that King and other ministers held rang with phrases from freedom songs.

> I got on my marching shoes!
> *Yes, Lord, me too.*
> I woke up this morning with my mind stayed on freedom!
> *Preach, doctor, preach*
> Some of you are afraid,
> *That's right, that's right.*
> But if you won't go . . . .
> *Don't hinder me*

Each volunteer for the demonstrations was trained in nonviolent techniques and asked to sign a commitment card, pledging to abide by the rules of nonviolent resistance. Persons who did not feel certain that they could remain nonviolent might choose to help with duties such as driving, manning telephones, mimeographing, typing, etc.

Phase two of Project C was planned to involve more people and heighten the drama. King addressed a mass meeting and gave a blueprint for gaining freedom in Birmingham: ". . . we must no longer spend our money in businesses that discriminate against Negroes. . . . Don't ever be afraid to die. . . . You must say somehow, 'I don't have much money. I don't have much education. I may not be able to read and write; but I do have the capacity to die.'"

The boycott, picketing, and sit-ins at department stores increased. Selection of the targets was masterminded by Reverend Wyatt Tee Walker, the young veteran of sit-ins and the Freedom Ride who had been appointed executive director of SCLC. Blacks in Birmingham, 40 percent of the population, represented great economic power. Profits dipped sharply when the boycott hit.

Police Chief Bull Connor steadfastly refused to issue a permit for the demonstrators to march peacefully. "No, you will not get a permit in Birmingham, Alabama to picket," he said. "I will picket you over to the city jail."

On Saturday, April 6, Shuttlesworth led about thirty people in a peaceful protest march to City Hall. Three blocks from their destination, Connor's officers stopped them with orders to disperse. The marchers refused in a polite manner. They were arrested and taken to jail on charges of "parading without a permit." Connor was trying hard to imitate the tactics of Chief Pritchett of Albany. He wanted to avoid any national publicity for King or the movement.

April 7 was Palm Sunday. A. D. King, Martin King's brother, led a march, wearing his surplice and carrying a Bible. A. D. was pastor of a Birmingham church. Hundreds of supporters lined the sidewalks and cheered. That was the day Connor ordered the dogs out. Policemen held the ferocious, snarling dogs on leashes. One command and the dogs would attack. The officers ordered the sympathizers to clear the sidewalks. They refused. Some began shouting back. In the excitement, one of the dogs lunged toward a black man and knocked him to the ground. Tension reached explosive pitch.

Three days later, the movement faced a serious crisis. King learned that city lawyers would seek a court order, or injunction, against all further demonstrations. Such injunctions had been used to stall protests in many cities. An appeal would only result in a lengthy lawsuit. Even if the movement won, the Birmingham campaign could be brought to a standstill.

King asked Wyatt Walker to call the television and press reporters. He had become a master at using news media to publicize high points of the freedom campaigns. That afternoon when a sheriff came to serve King with the injunction papers, reporters recorded the action. That was not all. King arranged for a press conference the next day, Holy Thursday.

By noon, twenty or more reporters were already waiting in the courtyard of the Gaston Motel, headquarters for the staff of Project C. The motel was owned by A. G. Gaston, the city's black millionaire. King, Abnernathy, and Shuttlesworth were seated at tables, facing a battery of television cameras set to transmit words and pictures. For conferences of this type, the ministers usually dressed in business suits and ties. This day they wore faded denim overalls and open-necked shirts—their "work clothes."

In his announcement, King told reporters, "We cannot in all good conscience obey such an injunction, which is unjust, undemocratic, and unconstitutional misuse of the legal process." After he read the entire statement, he answered questions from reporters. "Yes," he told them, "the direct action will continue today, tomorrow, Saturday, Sunday, and on through." One reporter wanted to know whether he would lead a march on Good Friday. King answered with an emphatic yes. "I am prepared to go to jail and stay as long as necessary." Abernathy and Shuttlesworth answered other questions as reporters scribbled notes.

Late Thursday evening, more distressing news threatened to upset King's plans. The bondsman who had furnished bail for jailed demonstrators told King he could not continue. City officials had informed him that his financial assets were not sufficient. Without bond money, demonstrators in jail would have to stay there. Without promise of bail, new volunteers would hesitate before demonstrating.

The Project C leaders met in Room 30 of the Gaston Motel to wrestle with possible solutions. "Martin," one of them said, "this means you can't go to jail. We need money. . . . You are the only one who has contacts to get it."

That day, Martin King stood at a crossroads. If he did not go to jail as he said he would, he could lose credibility. If he did go, he might be kept there so long that the movement might fail. King described later how "a sense of doom began to pervade the room." His staff looked to him for an answer.

King left the room to be alone and pray for guidance. "There comes a time in the atmosphere of leadership when a man surrounded by loyal friends and allies has to come face to face with himself," he wrote later. He thought about the three hundred volunteers waiting in jail. Then he thought about the millions of black Americans longing for justice. After that, as he recalled, "there was no more room for doubt." He put on his "work clothes" of blue denim trousers and gray shirt. His attire foretold his decision before he spoke: "I've got to march."

"That was, I think," wrote Andrew Young, "the beginning of his true leadership."

Shortly before noon the next day, Good Friday, the group drove to the Zion Hill Baptist Church. The fifty volunteers chosen to march formed a line, two abreast. King, Abernathy, and Al Hibbler, a blind black musician, moved into place at the head of the line. Slowly they marched toward City Hall. All along the way the people cheered and sang out, "Freedom has come to Birmingham!" Most of them were dressed in old clothes to symbolize their refusal to shop downtown for Easter finery.

After a few blocks police officers stopped the line. Bull Connor and Martin King stood face to face. Connor's temper suddenly exploded. He stomped about, his hat cocked over one eye, and bellowed commands. "Stop 'em!" Every movement registered fury.

King and Abernathy dropped to their knees in prayer. Photographers took pictures. One photo showed how policemen pulled the two ministers roughly by the seats of their pants and shoved them into waiting paddy wagons. With sirens blaring, the wagons sped toward the city jail.

King was placed in solitary confinement, his cell a narrow dungeon. There was a bunk, but no mattress, pillow, or blanket. Iron bars muted the sunlight. He was cut off from the world, not allowed to call his wife, or his attorney. He worried about Coretta and the new baby. He worried about Project C. Could his staff manage to raise the bail bond money?

Easter Sunday brought hope. Two attorneys were allowed to visit his cell for a brief time. The next day King learned that his friend Harry Belafonte had raised the needed bail bond money to free the demonstrators.

The jailers suddenly became considerate. They brought a mattress and pillow, and even allowed King to leave his cell for exercise. When they finally allowed him to telephone Coretta, he learned the reasons behind the sudden turnabout. Coretta, not knowing whether her husband was dead or alive, had called President Kennedy. Both John and Robert Kennedy opened up a hot line to Birmingham officials, who soon learned that the national spotlight was on them and how they were treating Martin King.

King's attorneys visited him on Tuesday; they brought a copy of the *Birmingham News*. It carried a letter, signed by eight white Birmingham ministers, attacking the civil rights demonstrations.

King read the letter carefully and decided that he would answer it. In the dim light of the cell he began to write.

Bull Connor's Jail

Down in Al - a - bam - a, In the
land of Jim Crow, There is a place where
Lots of folks go. Bir - ming - ham jail -
house, Bir - ming - ham jail, Wait - ing for
free - dom In Bull Con - nor's jail.

Three thousand prisoners,
    More coming in
Even little children
    Are singing this song.
Chorus

Bull Connor tells us
    "Don't raise a squawk
You need a permit
    Even to walk."
Chorus

Went to the church house
To sing and pray,
Started downtown and
They hauled us away.
Chorus

Pushed by policemen,
Herded like hogs
Some got the fire hose
And some got the dogs.
Chorus

Crammed in like sardines
In Bull Connor's can,
Some can lay down,
But others must stand.
Chorus

Iron bars around me
Cold walls so strong
They hold my body,
The world hears my song.
Chorus

In May 1963, the young people of Birmingham, Alabama staged their famous marches in protest against segregation in that city. Not only teenagers but tiny children dressed in their Sunday best were confronted by police dogs and fire hoses, and herded by the hundreds into the city jails. The brutality exhibited on this occasion by Bull Connor, Birmingham's tough director of "public security", led immediately to a national protest—the historic March on Washington of August 28. Guy and Candie Carawan were among those jailed. With the help of Ernie Marrs they rewrote "Down in the Valley" to suit the occasion. (Source: The Ballad of America by John A. Scott. Used by permission.)

The eight ministers had charged that the demonstrations were "directed in part by outsiders." "I am in Birmingham," King answered, "because injustice is here. . . . just as the Apostle Paul left his village of Tarsus and carried the gospel of Jesus Christ to the far corners of the Greco-Roman world, so am I compelled to carry the gospel of freedom beyond my own home town. . . . Injustice anywhere is a threat to justice everywhere. . . ."

The ministers had charged that the demonstrations were untimely. "We have waited," King told them, "for more than 340 years for our constitutional God-given rights. The nations of Asia and Africa are moving with jetlike speed toward political independence, but we creep at horse-and-buggy pace toward gaining a cup of coffee at a lunch counter. . . ."

The ministers charged that movement people, by defying segregation, were breaking the law. There is no obligation, King explained, to obey unjust laws that are "out of harmony with the moral law." Disobedience to unjust laws is obedience to God. "It was practiced superbly," he wrote, "by the early Christians who were willing to face hungry lions . . . rather than submit to certain unjust laws of the Roman Empire. . . ."

King went on to talk about his disappointment that Southern ministers of God should prefer order to justice. "I had hoped," he said, "that white moderates would understand that the present tension in the South is a necessary phase. . . ." Black people were unwilling to tolerate injustice any longer. The civil rights movement did not create the tension generated by injustice; it only brought it into the open. Where injustice existed and people struggled to end it, disorder would exist in the course of the effort to create a better world.

In their statement the white ministers had praised the Birmingham police for maintaining "order" and "preventing violence." "I wish," King told them, "you had commended the Negro sit-inners and demonstrators of Birmingham for their sublime courage, their willingness to suffer and their amazing discipline in the midst of great provocation. One day the South will recognize its real heroes. . . . They will be old, oppressed, battered Negro women . . . high school and college students . . . young ministers of the gospel. . . . One day the South will know that when these disinherited children of God sat down at lunch counters, they were in reality standing up for what is best in the American dream. . . ."

Black people in America, King concluded, will indeed win their freedom. "Abused and scorned though we may be, our

destiny is tied up with America's destiny. . . . If the inexpressible cruelties of slavery could not stop us, the oppression
we now face will surely fail. We will win our freedom because
the sacred heritage of our nation and the eternal will of God
are embodied in our echoing demands."

Smuggled out of jail, the *Letter from Birmingham Jail* was
printed as a pamphlet; a million copies went into circulation at
once. Instantly, it became a living document of American
history, destined to be read by future generations of
Americans as a part of their literary and moral heritage.

On Saturday, April 20, King and Abernathy posted bond
and left jail. Convicted later of criminal contempt, their
lawyers appealed; they remained free.

Now King and his staff began planning phase three of
Project C. This would be the critical and most dangerous seg-
ment of the direct action campaign. In his *Letter from
Birmingham Jail* King explained the need for this type of confrontation—"to create such a crisis and foster such a tension
that a community which has refused to negotiate is forced to
confront the issue. [Confrontation] seeks so to dramatize the
issue that it can no longer be ignored."

The plan was risky. It was daring. If it worked, the federal
government would no longer be able to ignore what was
going on in Birmingham, Alabama. It involved the use of
children. More than 6,000 elementary and high school
students were trained and ready. They had viewed films of the
sit-ins. They learned about mass action, and the possible
dangers involved. Diane Nash and James Bevel, now
married, worked miracles in getting youngsters psychologi-
cally ready for nonviolent action. All were eager to be involved. And, as Bevel explained, schoolchildren had no jobs,
and would not risk losing pay the way adults did. There was
another factor. If brutality was used against young people,
sympathy would swing toward the freedom campaign.

Still, King hesitated. "What are you going to do about the
children?" his staff kept asking. King, alone, had to answer,
for now and for history. If some of the youngsters got killed,
he would be severely censured. His reputation could be lost.

On the other hand, if Project C failed, hope for similar protests across the South would dim.

Martin King meditated and prayed over the matter for days. He finally based his decision upon a truth he often quoted: "In most of the direct action crusades, it had been the young people who sparked the movement."

Thursday, May 2, dawned hot and muggy in Birmingham. By noon, the Sixteenth Street Church was crowded with youngsters eager to march. Around 1:30 the first group moved through the church doors. The ages ranged from six to sixteen. Younger children had insisted that morning upon following older brothers and sisters. Singing songs of freedom, the youngsters marched in squads of twenty to thirty and took different routes leading toward City Hall. Bevel and adult marshals coordinated group movements with walkie-talkies.

The sight of hundreds of black children marching without fear sent Connor charging about and barking commands: "Get those little niggers!" Police officers filled up paddy wagons, and when they ran out, filled up school buses. By evening, nine hundred fifty-nine young people had been jailed, many in makeshift temporary quarters with poor sanitary facilities.

On the next day, two thousand five hundred students came to the church. King was there to inspire them. "Yesterday was D-Day in Birmingham," he said. "Today will be Double D-Day." He urged his young followers, "Don't get tired. Don't get bitter."

Once again the marching columns moved downtown, carrying bold signs that read "FREEDOM." A crowd of cheering bystanders watched them from Kelly Ingram Park, a tree-shaded square of greenery opposite Sixteenth Street Church. Meanwhile, Bull Connor had set up a barricade, with police officers, firemen with their trucks, and a corps of German police dogs, growling and straining at the leashes. When the young marchers neared this barricade, Connor made a fateful decision. He barked his favorite command for dealing with blacks: "Let 'em have it!"

The firemen, wearing slickers, opened their high pressure hoses. Jets of water, powerful enough to strip bark from trees, or skin from bodies, knocked marchers to the ground. Small children were swept into curbs or dashed against parked cars.

The bystanders became enraged. In defiance, some began to hurl whatever objects they could find. When Connor ordered the crowd to leave, they refused. Connor charged about in fury, his straw hat cocked, a cigar in his mouth. "Let 'em have it!" he ordered again. This time the dogs were unleashed. With fangs bared, they charged toward children and adults, tearing the clothes of some, severely biting many.

Newspapers printed the pictures and stories on front pages the next day. Americans watched the television pictures in disbelief. For the next two days the story was similar. Connor refused to back down, and the children refused to stop marching. "Join the thousands in jail who are making their witness for freedom," Bevel urged them in printed leaflets. "It's up to you to free our teachers, our parents, yourselves, and our country." And the children kept marching, shouting, "Freedom! Freedom! Freedom!"

Firemen use high pressure hoses on nonviolent demonstrators during the 1963 Birmingham demonstrations. (Charles Moore/ Black Star)

On Sunday, May 5, King spoke to a mass meeting. He told Birmingham's blacks, "As hard as it is, we must meet physical force with Soul Force. . . . We're struggling not to save ourselves alone, but we're struggling to save the soul of this nation."

On that same Sunday, an event took place that many people marked as a turning point in Project C. Reverend Charles Billups and other ministers led hundreds of young people in a pilgrimage to Birmingham jail. Connor ordered them to stop and retreat. The marchers refused to obey. Then suddenly Billups stood up in the manner of a biblical prophet and shouted: "We're not turning back. . . . Bring on your dogs. Beat us up. Turn on your hoses. We will stand here till we die." Connor then ordered the fire hoses opened. His officers obeyed, but no water came gushing out. There was a sudden loss of pressure in the nearby hydrant. The officers stood as though transfixed. The marchers moved on past them and knelt in prayers of thanksgiving. Someone cried out, "The Lord is with this movement. . . ."

By May 7th more than three thousand young people had been arrested. The sheriff reported that if the police continued to arrest demonstrators, the only facility large enough to hold them would be Birmingham's football stadium. There were four thousand still picketing and parading.

Burke Marshall, assistant attorney general for civil rights, was dispatched to Birmingham to work out an agreement. Other concerned Americans were working quietly behind the scenes. Religious leaders, North and South, called upon Birmingham ministers to preach racial harmony. Heads of businesses with Birmingham branches and chain-store executives urged desegregation. Birmingham's business leaders began seeking a compromise. With such display of goodwill, King declared a truce on demonstrations. Attorney General Robert Kennedy succeeded in getting major labor unions to donate money to pay the bail bond needed to free those who were in jail.

On May 10, King, Abernathy, and Shuttlesworth announced a "Birmingham Truce Agreement." It called for desegregation of lunch counters, fitting rooms, restrooms, and drinking fountains in downtown stores within ninety days. Within sixty days, there would be improved hiring practices, with black workers being considered for higher-paying jobs that had been closed to them. A vital part of the agreement established a biracial committee to forge communication between black and white citizens of Birmingham.

Martin King called the agreement, "the most significant victory for justice we've ever seen in the Deep South." He later wrote a book titled, *Why We Can't Wait,* and explained the Birmingham campaign. Because of it, he said, "the whole spectrum of the civil-rights struggle would undergo basic change. Nonviolence had passed the test of its steel in the fires of turmoil. The united power of Southern segregation was the hammer. Birmingham was the anvil."

8

THE BROADENING
FREEDOM MOVEMENT AND
THE MARCH ON WASHINGTON

On May 17, 1963 President Kennedy spoke to the nation. "Next week," he told his listeners, "I shall ask the Congress of the United States to act, to make a commitment it has not fully made in this century to the proposition that race has no place in American life. . . ." What he was asking for, he said, was a law giving all Americans "the right to be served in facilities which are open to the public." A new civil rights bill was sent to Congress on June 19.

Three days later the president met with Martin King, Philip Randolph, John Lewis, and other black leaders. They informed Kennedy that a march on Washington would be held to support the demand that Congress speedily debate and pass the law.

John Kennedy didn't like the idea. "If you bring that many people here," he asked, "how are we going to control them?"

Philip Randolph answered that black people were already in the streets everywhere, demonstrating for their rights. "Is it not better," he said, "that they be led by organizations disciplined by struggle? Mr. President, there will be a march!"

The president reluctantly agreed to support the demonstration; he assigned White House assistants to help work out the details.

Philip Randolph, director of the project, gave it its name: "The March on Washington for Jobs and Freedom." The march would take place on August 28. The message it would send to Congress would be that blacks and whites in America were united in their support for the civil rights bill and its speedy passage.

Bayard Rustin set to work as the march's chief organizer. Committees were set up in every state. Church, civic, and labor leaders recruited their followers across the nation to join the March. Dr. Anna Hedgeman, the first woman to serve on the mayor's cabinet in New York City, was the lone female member of the march's Executive Committee.

Rustin's plan called for tens of thousands of people to show up in the capital on August 28. There were all kinds of things that you had to think through, he said, "how many toilets you needed, where they should be. We had to consult doctors on exactly what people should bring to eat so that they wouldn't get sick. . . . We had to arrange for drinking water. We had to arrange what would happen if there was a terrible thunderstorm that day. We had to think of the sound system for the speakers."

By August the preparations had been made, the program set up, and the word spread: Washington, D.C. is where to be on August 28.

The people came, singing songs of freedom. In the early morning hours groups began to head toward the Washington Monument, where the assembly area was. By dawn trains and buses had begun to pour into the capital. One train came from the Deep South bringing farm people. Six buses brought people on a 22-hour trip from Birmingham. Four hundred buses poured in from Philadelphia alone. As for New York City, the people there had reserved every single bus that was available in the metropolitan area. By noon the highways into Washington were clogged with bumper-to-bumper traffic.

At the Washington Monument, stage and screen stars assembled upon a specially constructed platform to entertain the people while they waited for the march to begin. Some performers were famous, like Joan Baez, Bob Dylan, Odetta, Lena Horne, Marlon Brando, Sammy Davis, Jr. Others were unknowns, like a teenager who had faced police dogs and cattle prods in Alabama but brought his guitar with him to Washington. The air was vibrant with freedom songs, hymns, patriotic songs, ballads. James Baldwin, the famous black writer, stood on the platform gazing at the vast throng of humanity around him. He told how he felt: "I'd have to cry or sing," he said.

Reporters mingled with the crowd and wrote about what they saw. An eighty-two-year-old man made the trip on a bicycle; another man came on roller skates from Chicago—nearly 800 miles away. Aged or disabled people rolled along in wheelchairs, or walked on crutches.

The president was afraid of violence with so many people in D.C., and took his own precautions. Key federal buildings were locked and barred; helmeted troops occupied them and set up machine guns. An Army division, National Guard troops, and police officers were on stand-by alert. The march, too, had its own security forces, volunteers with bands around their arms, who acted as parade marshals.

All the precautions, as it turned out, were unnecessary, for the march was absolutely nonviolent. The marchers heeded well Rustin's appeal; "We are asking each person," he said, "to be a marshal of himself, since anybody who turns to violence will be a traitor to our cause."

Close to noon the march began. Moving slowly out from the assembly area the marchers streamed down Pennsylvania Avenue to the Lincoln Memorial, where the speakers would address them from the steps.

Those who walked linked arms with their neighbors. There were no strangers on August 28. Leaders of Catholic, Protestant, and Jewish faiths joined with white and black working people to demonstrate unity in support of the civil rights bill. Parents marched with little children on their shoulders, older ones by their sides. Hundreds had scrimped and saved for weeks in order to have enough money to make the trip. Workers sacrificed a day's pay to be there. In some parts of the South poor people pooled their funds so that one or two could go to represent many. Photographers took shots of the real America—interracial, interfaith, multicultural.

An ocean of placards bobbed about above the crowd, giving the message why the people were marching: DECENT HOUSING—NOW! JOBS FOR ALL—NOW! INTEGRATED SCHOOLS—NOW! FIRST-CLASS CITIZENSHIP—NOW!

At the Lincoln Memorial speakers and honored guests began to assemble, and waited for the crowd to gather. Seventy-five U.S. senators were placed in a reserved section near the speaker's stand. Women, too, held seats of honor on the platform. Coretta King was there; and so was Myrlie Evers. She was the widow of Medgar Evers, the World War II veteran and NAACP field secretary assassinated in front of his home in Mississippi in June. Diane Nash Bevel represented the young women of the Freedom Ride. Daisy Bates was there, leader of the Little Rock Nine. So was Rosa Parks, the seamstress from Montgomery who in 1955 summoned all of the black people of the South to do battle against segregation.

Marchers who arrived earliest at the Lincoln Memorial broke into small groups and picnicked on the grass. Some who had risen very early for the long trip to Washington began to snooze. Latecomers who could get nowhere near the Memorial could not hear everything that was said. It was enough to be there, to be part of the meaning and the enchantment of that extraordinary day.

At 1:30 Camilla Williams, black concert and opera star, sang the "Star Spangled Banner"; Rev. Fred Shuttlesworth of Birmingham gave the invocation. Asa Philip Randolph, seventy-four years of age, tall, straight, distinguished-looking, presided over the gathering. "We are gathered here," he said in his resonant, bass voice, "in the largest demonstration in the history of this nation."

In the heat of the day came the speeches, one after the other. Floyd McKissick of CORE, read a message from James Farmer. "From a South Louisiana jail," McKissick read, "I salute the March on Washington. . . . Two hundred and thirty freedom fighters here with me also send their greetings. . . ."

Youngest of the speakers was John Lewis, veteran of the sit-ins and the Freedom Rides. Just before the program was scheduled to begin, an offstage crisis had developed when the draft of Lewis' remarks was circulated among march leaders. Lewis did not endorse the civil rights bill, he said, because "it was too little and too late." He noted that there was absolutely nothing in the bill to authorize the federal government to protect civil rights fighters against police violence. "This bill," Lewis wanted to say, "will not protect young children and old women from police dogs and fire hoses . . ." The voting section of the bill, Lewis continued, "will not help thousands of black citizens who want to vote . . . What is in the bill that will protect the homeless and starving people of this nation?"

John Lewis was perfectly right. The bill would neither address nor solve all the problems of joblessness, poverty, racial violence, and votelessness that afflicted the black people. But March leaders were shocked when they read Lewis' words. His remarks, they thought, would mar the unity of the occasion. In a huddle hastily convened just before the meeting opened the SNCC leader was pressured to moderate his attack; reluctantly he gave in.

What Lewis said to the March audience was, instead, simply a statement of fact. "There are sharecroppers in the Delta of Mississippi who are in the fields working for less than three dollars a day, twelve hours a day. . . . The black masses are on the march for jobs and freedom. . . . And so, we have taken to the streets, . . ." He spoke with passion and sincerity and was loudly applauded.

The afternoon wore on. Mahalia Jackson, former hotel maid turned concert artist, came forward and sang an old spiritual that told of the deep pain of an oppressed people:

> I've been 'buked and I've been scorned,
> I've been talked about, sure's you born.

The shadows were lengthening; people at the edge of the huge crowd began to drift away. Philip Randolph introduced the last speaker of the day: Dr. Martin Luther King, Jr.

Dr. Martin Luther King, Jr. waves to the 250,000 people who cheer his speech at the March on Washington, August 28, 1963. (AP/Wide World)

He stood at the microphone, waiting for the tumult of cheering and applause to die down. At thirty-three he was slightly heavier than in the Montgomery days, but trim and handsome, still with an appealing look of vulnerability. He gazed out over the throng. The people, 250,000 of them, were spread before him on all sides. At the back they spilled over along both sides of the reflecting pool.

The audience became quiet; Martin King began to speak. "Five score years ago," he said, "a great American in whose symbolic shadow we stand, signed the Emancipation Proclamation. . . . But one hundred years later, we must face the tragic fact that the Negro is still not free." They had come to Washington, he told his audience, "to cash a check. When the architects of our republic wrote the magnificent words of the Constitution and the Declaration of Independence, they were signing a promissory note to which every American was to fall heir. This note was a promise that all men would be guaranteed the unalienable rights of life, liberty, and the pursuit of happiness."

As far as people of color were concerned, King went on, America had failed to honor that promise; instead it had given the Negro people a check that had bounced and been returned, marked "insufficient funds." But, said King, they didn't believe that justice in America is bankrupt. So they came back, he said, "to cash this check—a check that will give us upon demand the riches of freedom and the security of justice."

What exactly, he asked, does the citizen of color want?

Blacks, he said, would no longer tolerate the police brutality of which they were daily victims, nor denial of service in hotels and restaurants because of their color, nor denial of the vote, nor life in ghetto slums.

"I say to you today, my friends, that in spite of the difficulties and frustrations of the movement I still have a dream. . . . I have a dream that one day this nation will rise up and live out the true meaning of its creed: 'We hold these truths to be self-evident, that all men are created equal.'"

King had touched the deepest chord in the black soul. Blacks had always known that both in their own eyes and in the eyes of God they were as good as other people and ought to be treated as equals. But they adapted to the humiliations that the white man heaped upon them; they learned to be patient, and to wait. All the time, they went on dreaming, and nourishing their dream.

"I have a dream that one day on the red hills of Georgia the sons of former slaves and the sons of former slaveowners will be able to sit down together at the table of brotherhood. I have a dream that one day even the state of Mississippi, a desert state sweltering with the heat of injustice and oppression, will be transformed into an oasis of freedom and justice. I have a dream that my four little children will one day live in a nation where they will not be judged by the color of their skin but by the content of their character.

"I have a dream today.

"I have a dream that one day every valley will be exalted, every hill and mountain shall be made low, the rough places will be made plain, and the crooked places will be made straight, and the glory of the Lord shall be revealed, and all flesh shall see it together.

"This is our hope. This is the faith I shall return to the South with. . . . With this faith we will be able to work together, pray together, struggle together, go to jail together, stand up for freedom together, knowing that we will be free one day."

One day, he went on, all of God's children in America would be able to sing with new meaning the old familiar song

> My country 'tis of thee
> Sweet land of liberty, of thee I sing.
> Land where my fathers died,
> Land of the pilgrims' pride,
> From every mountainside
> Let freedom ring.

Now he came to the climax of his speech.

"Let freedom ring from the prodigious hilltops of New Hampshire . . . from the mighty mountains of New York . . . from the heightening Alleghenies of Pennsylvania . . . from the snow-capped Rockies of Colorado . . . from the curvaceous slopes of California . . . from Stone Mountain of Georgia . . . from Lookout Mountain of Tennessee. Let freedom ring from every hill and molehill of Mississippi . . . let freedom ring."

When we work, struggle, and die for freedom, he said, and strive to make it real in every hamlet, village, city, and state in the land, we bring closer the day when "all of God's children,

black men and white men, Jews and Gentiles, Protestants and
Catholics, will be able to join hands and sing in the words of
the old spiritual, 'Free at last! Free at Last! Thank God
Almighty, we are free at last!'"

9

ST. AUGUSTINE, FREEDOM SUMMER AND THE NOBEL PEACE PRIZE, 1964

It was Sunday, September 15, just eighteen days after the March on Washington. Worshippers were arriving at Birmingham's Sixteenth Street Baptist Church, a rallying place for the Children's Crusade earlier in the summer. Children were in their Sunday school classes, dressed in white for the annual Youth Day. There was a roar as dynamite exploded, tearing away the rear wall of the church. Stone and glass rained down.

"Lie down on the floor!" Sunday school teachers screamed. For four children it was too late. Addie Mae Collins, Carole Robertson, Cynthia Wesley, and Denise McNair lay dead. Twenty-one others were injured.

There was rage in the Birmingham streets, and in other cities of the South. Some wept, or cursed. Others pelted police cars after officers killed a black youth. Many swore that they wanted nothing more to do with nonviolence, that they would have vengeance upon the murderers. President Kennedy spoke to the nation: ". . . it is not too late for all concerned to unite in steps toward peaceful progress before more lives are lost."

Birmingham Sunday

Slowly

Come round by my side and I'll sing you a song. I'll sing it so soft-ly, it-'ll do no one wrong — On Bir-ming-ham Sun-day the blood ran like wine, And the choirs kept sing-ing of Free-dom—

Come round by my side, and I'll sing you a song,
I'll sing it so softly it'll do no one wrong:
On Birmingham Sunday the blood flowed like wine,
    And the choir kept singing of freedom.

That cold autumn morning no eye saw the sun,
And Addie May Collins her number was one,
In an old Baptist Church there was no need to run,
    And the choir kept singing of freedom.

The clouds they were dark and the autumn wind blew,
And Denise McNair brought the number to two,
The falcon of death was a creature she knew,
    And the choir kept singing of freedom.

The Church it was crowded and no one could see
That Cynthia Wellesley's number was three,
Her prayers and her feelings would shame you and me,
    And the choir kept singing of freedom.

Young Carol Roberts then entered the door,
And the number her killers had given was four,
She asked for a blessing and asked for no more,
    And the choir kept singing of freedom.

On Birmingham Sunday a noise shook the ground,
And people all over the earth turned around,
For no one recalled a more cowardly sound,
    And the choir kept singing of freedom.

The Sunday has come and the Sunday has gone,
And I can't do much more that to sing you a song,
I'll sing it so softly it'll do no one wrong,
    And the choir keeps singing of freedom.

Soon after the tragedy of September 15 Richard Farina composed this ballad and set it to an ancient Scottish melody, "I Once Loved a Lass." "Birmingham Sunday" is remembered as one of the most beautiful of many songs composed by talented song writers during the 1960s. ("Birmingham Sunday" by Richard Farina. Copyright 1964 Vogue Music (c/o The Welk Music Group, Santa Monica, CA 90401). International Copyright Secured. All rights reserved. Used by permission.)

As for Martin King, he praised the dead girls as "heroines of a holy crusade for freedom and human dignity." The bombing made him more determined to work even harder to banish the atmosphere of hatred and to create a climate of peace.

The young people of SNCC, who had endured so much for human rights, wanted more than words. They called for massive demonstrations on a national scale. After discussions with Birmingham and national black leaders, King sided with the recommendation to plan more far-reaching campaigns that would seek to end the bigotry that resulted in murderous acts. This decision caused a rejection of King's leadership style and philosophy by many young people who were losing faith in the power of nonviolence to bring equality in the South.

Two months later President Kennedy was assassinated in Dallas, Texas. Vice President Lyndon Baines Johnson was at once sworn in as the thirty-sixth president. On November 27, in his first presidential speech to Congress, he said, "We have talked for one hundred years or more. Yes, it is time to write the next chapter and to write it in books of laws." Johnson put the weight of his influence behind passage of the civil rights bill. A few days later he scheduled a conference with King and the two talked together for nearly an hour.

The twelve months Martin King called "the most decisive year in the Negro's fight for equality" came to a close. It was decisive for King also, according to editors of *Time* magazine, for they named him "Man of the Year." "Few can explain the extraordinary King mystique," the *Time* salute stated. "Yet he has an indescribable capacity for empathy that is the touchstone of leadership."

In early March 1964, King went to Orlando, Florida to help organize a Florida SCLC affiliate. While there he learned how Dr. Robert Hayling, a dentist, was leading a protest movement in St. Augustine, site of America's oldest settlement. White officials of St. Augustine had applied for a federal grant to plan a four hundredth anniversary celebration in 1965. All festivities would be segregated. Even though blacks made up one-third of the population, none had jobs as policemen or firemen.

King promised help and sent two SCLC staff members. Hosea Williams, known as a nervy guy, had recently led a successful demonstration in Savannah, Georgia. Bernard Lee, jailed with King during the Atlanta sit-ins, was equally tough. Andrew Young, Fred Shuttlesworth, and C. T. Vivian joined them later. All were ministers.

By then, students and ministers were responding to letters from Dr. Hayling asking them to come to St. Augustine during the spring break. These outsiders joined the marches and sit-ins that were trying to open up facilities in "The Ancient City." The St. Augustine campaign offered King a classic confrontation to bring the issue of states' rights versus rights guaranteed by the federal courts out into the open. Under states' rights, Deep South states continued to exploit and intimidate blacks at will, while the federal officials made no attempt to intervene.

The symbolic rallying place for protest demonstrations was the old Slave Market in the town square. There, slaves had once been auctioned off to buyers like cattle. All that spring, Northern supporters continued to join the protest groups.

One of them was the socially prominent Mrs. Malcolm Peabody, wealthy, civic-minded mother of the governor of Massachusetts. When she was arrested, national news services gave more publicity to the St. Augustine campaign.

As daytime heat grew intense, rallies at the Slave Market were held at night. On the third night, the Ku Klux Klansmen attacked the marchers. They used all the bricks they had been storing up for days, plus any other weapons they could find. The police stood by, offering no help to the victims. One brutally beaten marcher said, "It's a miracle no one was killed." Hosea Williams talked later about the pride the once fearful blacks felt in being able to stand up to vicious beatings and remain nonviolent. Andrew Young recalled the courage it took "when you have one man, wearing civilian clothes, beating you while another, wearing a badge, stands waiting to arrest you when the first one gets tired. . . ."

On June 25, a Klan organizer from California led a rally. He preached, "I favor violence to preserve the white race, anytime, any place, anywhere. Now it may be some niggers are gonna get killed in the process, but when war's on, that's what happens."

When Martin King came to lead a rally, he talked of death in a different way. "Well, if physical death is the price I must pay to free my white brother and all my brothers and sisters from a permanent death of the spirit, then nothing can be more redemptive," he said. He told the people to sing the old slave song with new spirit:

> Before I'll be a slave
> I'll be buried in my grave

King was jailed for leading a march to integrate an exclusive motor lodge. After two days he was released on bail, in time to accept an honorary degree from Yale University. During the presentation ceremony, Yale President Kingman Brewster praised the apostle of nonviolence for "eloquence that has kindled the nation's sense of outrage."

This sense of outrage jolted President Johnson into faster action on the pending civil rights bill. The House of

Oh, Freedom!

Oh,— free-dom! oh,— free-dom!

Oh, free-dom o-ver me; And be-

fore I'll be a slave, I'll lie

bur-ied in my grave, And go

home to my Lord and — be free.

No more moaning, no more moaning,
No more moaning over me;
And before I'll be a slave,
I'll lie buried in my grave,
And go home to my Lord, and be free.

No more mourning, no more mourning,
No more mourning over me;
And before I'll be a slave, etc.

No more weeping, no more weeping,
No more weeping over me;
And before I'll be a slave, etc.

No more sighing, no more sighing,
No more sighing over me;
And before I'll be a slave, etc.

Oh, what singing, oh, what singing,
Oh, what singing over me;
And before I'll be a slave, etc.

This song was born during the Civil War, when black soldiers fought for their people's freedom and for the Stars and Stripes. It ranks among the great freedom songs of the civil rights movement. (Source: The Ballad of America *by John A. Scott. Used by permission.)*

Representatives used only eleven days to debate and clear the bill. In the Senate, however, it was a tough battle. When the time came to vote on closing debate, to cut off filibustering (cloture), all senators knew the vote would be close. Senator Clare Engel of California, dying and unable to speak, managed to point to his eye to record an "aye" vote. That day, for the first time in American history, the Senate evoked cloture on a civil rights bill. It passed on July 19, 1964.

Two veteran senators, Hubert Humphrey of Minnesota, a civil rights advocate, and Everett Dirksen of Illinois, a moderate, led the fight for passage. When Dirksen was asked why he, not known for civil rights activities, had done so, he quoted the French poet-dramatist Victor Hugo: "No army can withstand the strength of an idea whose time has come."

Hosea Williams gave credit to the determined protest movements by blacks in the South. "The Civil Rights Act was written in Birmingham," he said, "and passed in St. Augustine."

President Johnson invited King and other black leaders to witness the bill signed into law on July 2. From the East Ballroom of the White House, Johnson spoke over national radio and television. He said, ". . . those who are equal before God shall now be equal in the polling booths, in the classrooms, in the factories, and in hotels, restaurants, movie theaters, and other places that provide service to the public."

The president met with King and the black leaders after the signing. There was no need for further demonstrations in the streets, he advised them. Johnson planned to run for president in the next election, and he wanted calm in the country.

The Civil Rights Act of 1964 was the most sweeping ever passed. It now became an offense not to receive and serve black people at public accommodations—like hotels, restaurants, libraries—on the same basis as whites. The Act established a federal commission to ensure equal employment opportunities, and it made it an offense to deny anybody a job solely upon the basis of that person's color. But, as John Lewis had tried to tell the people at the March on Washington, the act did not go nearly far enough. It failed to provide ways for federal enforcement of black voting rights. There were no provisions to protect black people from violence when they were peacefully petitioning and demonstrating for their rights.

The right to vote had been written into the law by the Fifteenth Amendment in 1870: the amendment stated that "the right of citizens of the United States to vote shall not be denied or abridged by the United States or any State on account of race, color, or previous condition of servitude." But the amendment had long remained a dead letter, ignored by white Southerners, forgotten by federal officials. To revive it had remained a top priority for Martin King throughout his career; he recognized the ballot as the key to political power. It was the theme of his first national speech at the Prayer Pilgrimage in 1957. With voting rights, he said, blacks would be able to put people into power who would obey their will and work to satisfy their needs. They would no longer have to march in the streets and "vote with their feet."

Voter-education projects were being developed by young SNCC workers across the Deep South. Funds from philanthropic foundations made it possible to train volunteers as leaders who went back into their communities to conduct workshops on voting. In Mississippi, SNCC, CORE, SCLC, and the NAACP joined with local civil rights groups to form the Council of Federated Organizations (COFO). This organization developed a voting project under the leadership of a philosophical young black man named Robert Parris Moses. Born in Harlem and educated at Harvard, Moses left his position as mathematics teacher in New York and went to Mississippi to work for SNCC. His classic features, with freckles near his nose, soon became well-known all over the state.

Bob Moses organized a mock election he called the "Freedom Vote." It gave black citizens who had never voted the chance to practice casting their ballot. It also proved that blacks wanted to vote and would have great political clout because of their numbers. Mississippi had the highest ratio of blacks, nearly half the population. It also had the lowest percentage of black voters. Even when blacks risked violence and tried to register, they were disqualified on one pretext or another. Only 5 percent of the total black population had been registered.

The Freedom Vote was open to all races. Moses persuaded over sixty white students from Yale and Stanford universities to come and help organize the mock election. At least 93,000 persons voted in booths set up in beauty parlors and barbershops, on sidewalk tables, and other available places. Aaron Henry, a black pharmacist and state president of the NAACP, was elected as governor in the Freedom election. His running mate, the Reverend Edwin King, a white chaplain at all-black Tougaloo College, was elected lieutenant governor.

Moses supervised another creative project in 1964. When he first went to Mississippi in 1960 to recruit for the newly organized SNCC, he met an amazing man named Amzie Moore. This black businessman was described as "solid as a rock." One day the two sat at a pine table in a farmhouse and dreamed: What would happen if hundreds of young people from the North were brought to Mississippi for a summer? Out of this dream grew the Mississippi Summer Project, better known as Freedom Summer.

Moses recruited on large college campuses and explained the three objectives of the summer project: Voter registration, Freedom Schools, and community centers where poor people could get free medical help and legal service.

College students by the hundreds volunteered; three-fourths of them were white. The National Council of Churches funded training sessions at Western College for Women in Oxford, Ohio. Parents of these dedicated young people could not comprehend why their children would want to go to help blacks they did not even know. One young girl wrote to help her parents understand, saying, ". . . convictions are worthless in themselves, . . . if they don't become actions. . . ."

With this broadened awareness, the young people approached Freedom Summer with the determination of evangelists, bent on bringing hope and changing hearts.

Mississippi segregationists got ready for them. The mayor of Jackson, the state capital, hired extra police and bought more firearms and paddy wagons. He set up makeshift prisons, just in case they were needed.

The first group of volunteers left for Mississippi on June 20, 1964. The next day three civil rights workers disappeared. They had gone to check on the burning of a black church. James Chaney, a Mississippi native, was a CORE staff member. Andrew Goodman, a student from Queens College, had been in Mississippi less than twenty-four hours. Michael Schwerner, a social worker from New York, worked with CORE. Chaney was black. Goodman and Schwerner were white.

The mysterious disappearance caused a national uproar. Citizens demanded answers. The president authorized two hundred Navy men to join the search. FBI Director J. Edgar Hoover opened an office in Jackson and personally directed the efforts of one hundred fifty agents.

Goodman, Schwerner, and Chaney were almost certainly dead. But this did not stop the volunteers from pouring into Mississippi. They spread out over the lovely Magnolia State. Putting aside their college clothes, they donned cotton skirts, jeans, and overalls. They lived among the poor, often in unpainted or tarpaper shacks. They chopped weeds and shucked corn under the relentless burning sun, and helped with whatever their host families had to do. Those working on voter registration went into the communities and gained the confidence of the people; then they talked them into trying to register.

Other volunteers taught in Freedom Schools. More than two thousand black students came to these schools, which were held in churches or wherever space could be found. The children studied French, wrote plays, recited poetry, and discussed exciting stories about the lives of black heroes. Community centers were set up and proved as popular as the schools. Volunteer doctors came for periodic visits; lawyers did likewise.

Most of the visiting Northern students felt completely at home with the black families with whom they lived. "Whatever small bit we did for Mississippi this summer," wrote one, "Mississippi did ten times as much for us. . . . In Mississippi I have felt more love, more sympathy and warmth, more community, than I have known in my life."

The feeling was mutual. An old woman said, "They didn't mind dyin'." Amzie Moore had another thought. "They treated us like we were special," he said, "and we loved 'em."

On August 3, Pete Seeger, the popular folksinger, gave a concert in Meridian. He brought sad news. FBI agents had discovered the bodies of Chaney, Schwerner, and Goodman buried beneath an earthen dam near Philadelphia, Mississippi. The three had been arrested by the deputy sheriff of Philadelphia and turned over to the KKK, then shot to death, and buried beneath the dam with a bulldozer.

Many of the summer workers decided that they would stay on in Mississippi in honor of the three who had been slain. They wrote home to their families and told them that college would have to wait another term. The students knew well that there would still be shots through windows, jailings on phoney charges, rough living without modern conveniences. These were a small price to pay for what Ella Baker had urged them to fight for when she came to visit them in Mississippi— "freedom of the human spirit."

That summer Bob Moses spearheaded the organization of the Mississippi Freedom Democratic Party (MFDP), which enabled thousands of black people who were unable to nominate or vote for regular Democratic Party candidates to elect their own "freedom" delegates and send them to the Democratic National Convention in Atlantic City. When they arrived at the convention late in August the MFDP people went before the Credentials Committee and challenged the right of the white delegates to be seated at the convention. Those delegates, they charged, had been illegally chosen; blacks in Mississippi were totally excluded from the voting process. With borrowed badges they moved into the convention and occupied the seats of the white Mississippi delegates. When the seats were removed they stood in the empty spaces.

The MFDP challenge to the all-white Mississippi Democratic Party was carried live on TV. People watched an unlikely star, a stocky, forty-seven-year-old woman with soft, beautiful eyes, a former sharecropper. Fannie Lou Hamer, except for being born in a state that condemned her to poverty, might have been one of the world's great actresses. Her deep emotional voice, her presence, and her sheer guts, captivated the world. When she testified before the Credentials Committee, she told how she was fired from the plantation where she had been a sharecropper for eighteen years for daring to register as a voter. After that, she said, she "became a part of the nonviolent revolution." In her rhythmic style of speech, which filled the room as though she were singing the blues, she dramatized the indomitable will of black people to survive. The plight of all Mississippi blacks was heard through the melody of Fannie Lou Hamer.

Martin King lobbied and testified on behalf of MFDP. So did Roy Wilkins, and so did Rita Schwerner, widow of the slain civil rights worker. In the end, MFDP was offered two symbolic seats at the convention. The question of whether to accept this token was threshed out in an emotional meeting in a church near the convention center. King and Rustin were with the group that felt the compromise should be accepted. The Democrats had promised changes with the next election. Fannie Lou Hamer gave the view of the more militant delegates: "We didn't come all this way for no two seats."

The incident drove a deeper wedge between King's leadership and the more militant of SNCC. The younger people felt that King was far too moderate in his decisions.

Knowing this, King felt depressed. He had been on a treadmill of activity all summer long. He had made a tour of Mississippi to raise funds and publicize the work of the student volunteers. He had gone from one big city to another where riots broke out in poverty-ridden ghettos. There seemed no end to problems.

Exhausted mentally and physically, he took Coretta's advice and checked into a hospital in October for examination. Early the next morning, Coretta telephoned. Her voice sang out the news circling the world: Dr. Martin Luther King, Jr. had won the Nobel Peace Prize. At age thirty-five, he was the youngest person ever to receive the prize, awarded each year "for the most effective work in the interest of international peace." King announced that the prize money of $54,000 would be donated to carry on the Freedom Movement.

On December 4, the Kings, accompanied by a party of twenty-six, left for Norway. During impressive ceremonies on December 10, 1964 in Aula Hall of Oslo University, Dr. Martin Luther King, Jr., looking unusually young and handsome in formal attire, accepted the Peace Prize. Dr. Gunnar Jahn, head of the Peace Prize Committee, praised King as "the first person in the Western world to have shown us that a struggle can be waged without violence."

In his acceptance speech, King said, in part, "I accept this award today with an abiding faith in America and an audacious faith in the future of mankind." He gave recognition to the millions he represented, who would never rate a headline. "Yet when the years have rolled past and when the blazing light of truth is focused upon this marvelous age in which we live, men and women will know and children will be taught that we have a finer land, a better people, a more noble civilization, because these humble children of God are willing to suffer for righteousness' sake."

10

THE SELMA PROTEST AND THE VOTING RIGHTS ACT, 1965

L ate in 1964 when Martin King was preparing to go to Norway to accept the Nobel Peace Prize, he received an appeal from a committee of black leaders in Selma, Alabama. They were urging him to come to Selma in order to support their campaign for voting rights. His presence, they said, would bring national publicity; it would also inspire more people to join in protest marches to the courthouse. King sent members of the SCLC staff to Selma to work with the SNCC people who were already there to plan for the launching of the campaign early in 1965.

Martin King chose to commit himself to Selma because it was the right struggle at the right time. A voting rights campaign in 1965 would have national significance. The 1964 Civil Rights Bill, important as it was, contained no provision to deal with the disenfranchisement of which black citizens, especially in the Deep South, were victims. When blacks tried to register to vote at the courthouses, they were usually turned away on one pretext or another. Those who were bold enough to challenge this treatment, who refused to take "no" for an answer, faced violence. They might be thrown down the courthouse steps, beaten, or even killed.

Ever since 1957, when he led the Prayer Pilgrimage to Washington, voting rights had been one of Martin King's top priorities. He understood only too well that citizens without the vote were citizens without power both to write their demands into the programs of the political parties and to make sure that those demands were carried out. Yet another law was needed in order to fulfill the promise that the federal government had made in 1870, when the Fifteenth Amendment was written into the Constitution. The amendment stated that the right to vote would be denied to no citizen on account of "race, color, or previous condition of servitude." For nearly one century this promise had remained forgotten and ignored.

King expressed his concern to President Lyndon Johnson. The president told him face-to-face that there was absolutely no chance of getting another civil rights bill through Congress so soon after the passage of the 1964 bill.

This was why it was time to go back to the people in the streets, to begin another round of struggle.

Selma, in Dallas County, Alabama, was the right place to launch the new campaign. In Dallas County over 57 percent of the people were black, but only 1 percent of those eligible to vote were registered on the rolls. SNCC workers came to Dallas in 1962 and initiated a voter-education project; they held classes and urged black citizens to go down to the courthouse in groups and seek to register. Progress was very slow because, as in the past, most of the applicants were turned away. Local registrars, like the one in Selma, had a lot of power. They could simply say to a black person who came to register "Sorry, you don't pass the qualifying test." And that was that.

When Martin King arrived in Selma in January 1965, the nonviolent campaign was ready to begin and Selma's white lawpeople were ready for the campaigners. The mayor, Joseph Smitherman, didn't want any disorder or violence that would give the city a negative image. He hoped to attract new businesses to Selma that would give a lift to its sagging

economy. Law officers, he said, were to be on their best behavior. He appointed J. Wilson Baker, a tall, mild-mannered,
and moderate sort of person, as commissioner of public
safety.

The mayor's problem lay with the sheriff of Dallas County,
James (Jim) Clark, who was a different type of man. Jim Clark
was a notorious bully. Tipping the scales at 220 pounds and
dressed in a military-type uniform with braid-brimmed hat,
he swaggered around the courthouse intimidating black
citizens who dared to try and register. In his hatred and contempt for black people and civil rights workers Clark rivaled
Birmingham's Bull Connor.

Two little girls who lived in the George Washington Carver
Housing Project near Brown Chapel related their memories
of the Selma struggle to a Birmingham newspaperman, Frank
Sikora. Sikora recorded what they said and published it in
Selma, Lord, Selma, a best-seller.

Sheyann Webb, called Shey for short, was eight years old
that January when King came to Selma. She was the youngest
of eight children. Her mother had a job sewing shirts in a
factory; her father was a laborer. Shey was in the third grade.
She had a happy smile, beautiful hair, large brown twinkling
eyes, and tilt-up nose. She became interested in all the activity
around Brown Chapel, a redbrick church with twin steeples.
One morning she sat in the back of the church, watching what
was going on, and forgot to go to school. From that time the
Selma protest became for her the most important thing in the
world. More than once she was late for school.

Interest in the protest was shared by her best friend, nine-
year-old Rachel West, who attended Catholic Mission
School. Rachel's parents had joined with other families who
housed King's aides when they needed a place to stay. One
Sunday night Shey and Rachel dressed in their best clothes,
with ribbons in their hair, and sang freedom songs at a mass
meeting. From that night the little girls became a featured part
of the church rallies.

On Monday, January 18, King and John Lewis led would-
be voters to the county courthouse. Sheyann was there,
scared, and holding tight to the hand of the lady who marched

Two young civil rights demonstrators, Sheyann Webb and Rachel West, with Dr. King during the Selma Campaign, 1965. (Vernon Merritt/Black Star)

beside her. She recalled, "It occurred to me then that on this day at any moment after the first step, somebody might die." There would be no deaths, and no arrests that first day. Sheriff Clark kept his anger in check. He led the group to an alley entrance to the courthouse, instructing them to wait there until registrars called them one at a time to take the complicated test. Hours passed and not a single person was called.

On Tuesday, January 19, fifty volunteers tried again to register. They refused to be herded toward the alley entrance. When Clark ordered them to move from the pavement they took their time. Clark then grabbed a woman by her collar and pushed her half a block to his patrol car. It happened that the person he manhandled was Mrs. Amelia Boynton, a popular civic worker, businesswoman, and longtime activist. Many major newspapers published the photos that showed the sheriff in the brutal act of using his billy club against a leading citizen whose only crime was that she wanted to vote.

The movement quickened in pace after that. Waves of volunteers went to the courthouse and insisted on entering through the front door. King shuttled in and out of the city and monitored events by telephone. During one of his trips back to Selma, Rachel and Sheyann had the chance for a personal talk with him. They ran up behind him; he turned around to shake their hands.

"What do you want" he leaned down and whispered.

"Freedom," the little girls answered.

"That's what we all want," King assured them. The question and answer game became a ritual for King and the children. Sometimes at rallies he would let them sit on his knees while he waited to speak. Rachel remembered, "We'd be sitting up there so proud!" All during his speeches they watched him, fascinated. "I just enjoyed even looking at him, besides listening to him," Sheyann said.

On Friday, January 22, Selma citizens saw an astounding spectacle. Andrew Durgan and Rev. Frederick Reese, both teachers, led more than one hundred five black teachers who walked as a group to the courthouse late that afternoon. Some held up toothbrushes, boldly symbolizing a willingness to go to jail for freedom. The school board chairman and the superintendent of schools confronted them at the courthouse steps. So did Clark. "Do you have business in this courthouse?" he asked. "The only business we have here is to come to the Board of Registrars to register," a teacher answered. "You have one minute to get off these steps or I'll move you," Clark warned. Standing nearby and itching to help were the sheriff's possemen, most of them Klansmen, dressed in an assortment of clothes but each wearing on his helmet of whatever description the words in black letters: "Sheriff's posse."

The seconds ticked away. The teachers stood their ground. Andrew Young looked on and described the confrontation: "The most significant thing that has happened in the racial movement since Birmingham."

A black news reporter ran to a telephone and relayed the news. "I can't believe it," he shouted. "This is bigger than Lyndon Johnson coming to town."

It *was* big news. Never in any of the major civil rights campaigns had teachers demonstrated forcefully as a group.

The news reached students, who came running and shouting for joy: "The teachers are marching! The teachers are marching!" As the teachers walked triumphantly to Brown Church, students called out names when they saw their favorites.

Shey's teacher saw her and, wiping away tears, hugged her student. "You did real good!" Shey whispered.

Other groups followed the example set by the teachers. The undertakers marched together. So did the beauticians. Others followed. "Everybody marched after the teachers marched," Rev. Reese noted. SCLC workers phrased the excitement differently: "Brother, we got a movement going on in Selma!"

During another march a fifty-three-year-old demonstrator furnished another of the many anecdotes that gave courage and kept a movement alive. On Monday, January 25, King led a demonstration to the courthouse. Sheriff Clark strode up and down, now wearing on his lapel a large button showing the word "NEVER!" Mrs. Annie Lee Cooper, heavy-set and determined, looked at him and called out, "There ain't nobody scared around here." Clark's control snapped. He pushed Mrs. Cooper so hard she lost her balance. Her strong arms struck back. She slugged the sheriff to his knees, punched him again and jabbed her elbows into his stomach. Several of Clark's deputies then held her down while Clark beat her repeatedly with his club. Reporters trained their cameras on the action. Their photos of Clark beating the woman while deputies held her down publicized the growing crisis in Selma. The mood of the black community had changed. The people were now ready "to die on their feet rather than live on their knees."

King sensed the change and knew the time had come to shift to another phase of the protest. The moment for what he called "creative tension" had come. It was time for him to let himself be arrested. This would put more pressure on President Johnson to take action on the much-needed voting rights bill.

February 1 was declared Freedom Day in Selma. On that cold, drizzly morning Martin King faced the crowd at Brown Chapel, saying, "Whatever it takes to get the right to vote in this state we're going to follow that course. . . ." Together with Abernathy, he led two hundred sixty persons toward the courthouse. They marched in one, uninterrupted line instead of moving in small clusters of people as a city ordinance required. Public Safety Director Wilson Baker drove to meet them after a few blocks. "You will have to break up into small groups," he said.

"We feel that we have a constitutional right to walk down to the courthouse," King answered politely.

King, Abernathy, and other demonstrators were taken to jail. They refused to post bail so that they might be set free. King knew that his arrest would publicize conditions in the city and the state.

The publicity soon came. Selma had arrested a Nobel Peace Prize winner for the crime of leading citizens to register for the vote. On February 5 a congressional deelegation left D.C. for Selma. Demonstrations continued. The Dallas County jails overflowed with black protesters. Reporters and TV crews began to arrive. King wrote to Andy Young from jail. "Keep the pressure up," he said; "in a crisis we must have a sense of drama."

Then he drew up a letter to the citizens of America and had it printed in the *New York Times* as a full-page advertisement. "Have you ever," he asked the readers, "stood in line with over one hundred others [to register to vote] and after waiting an entire day seen less than ten given the qualifying test? This is Selma, Alabama," he went on, "*there are more Negroes in jail with me than there are on the voting rolls.*"

Coretta King and Juanita Abernathy came to Selma to be near their husbands while in jail and to help SCLC staff carry on the many tasks to be done. One night when Coretta arrived at Brown Chapel, Andy Young met her with surprising news. Malcolm X, at the invitation of SNCC, had arrived to address the audience.

Malcolm X was one of the youngest and the most able of black American leaders. Born Malcolm Little in Michigan, he dropped out of school as a teenager, hustled a living on the Harlem streets selling drugs, ended up in a Boston prison. He became attracted to the Black Muslims, who preached strict discipline and race pride. He used his prison time to read widely in American history and to educate himself. A man of brilliant intellect and a speaker of enormous power who could entrance and teach his audiences with prose of luminous beauty and simplicity, Malcolm's thinking had undergone continuous change. Beginning with beliefs in black power, separatism, and vengeance against whites, he had little use in the early 1960s for Martin King's nonviolent, love-thine-enemy approach. But a trip to Mecca brought home to him that Islam embraced peoples of all races. In his own way and in his own time he was coming to many of the same conclusions about race relations in America that King had already reached. Malcolm had gone to the March on Washington in 1963 in order to scoff. He came now to Selma for a different reason.

That night Malcolm X spoke in Brown Chapel. He told the audience he believed that a person had a right to use any means necessary to get the right to vote. Coretta talked with him after the meeting and was deeply impressed. She later wrote of his obvious intelligence and his gentleness. Malcolm told Coretta that he had hoped to visit King in jail. "I want Dr. King to know," he said to her, "that I didn't come to Selma to make his job difficult. I really did come thinking that I could make it easier. If the white people realize what the alternative is, perhaps they will be more willing to listen to Dr. King."

Less than three weeks later Malcolm was assassinated while he addressed an assembly in a Harlem ballroom. News of his death saddened Martin much; he had met Malcolm only once, and wished that the two had known each other better. "Malcolm X," he reflected, "was reevaluating his own philosophical suppositions and moving toward a greater understanding of the nonviolent movement and toward more tolerance of white people."

On Friday, February 5, King accepted bail and left the jail to meet with the congressional delegation. Four days later he flew to Washington to see administration officials, including Vice President Hubert Humphrey and, briefly, the president himself. At last, the Selma project had the attention of the White House, but as yet not enough to make it a top priority.

Events in rapid succession changed the picture. On February 10, a group of students staged another of their peaceful marches. As they lined up at the courthouse, Sheriff Clark shouted, "Left face!" The students turned. "March!" Clark ordered. Clark's deputies began pushing youngsters with clubs toward a prison work camp. "You wanted to march, so march!" they ordered. Riding in cars and trucks, they dangled electric cattle prods out of the windows and forced the young people to trot three miles. When any of them stopped, gasping for breath, the prodders jolted them into movement. The students limped back home when the police finally let them go. Many were sick from the ordeal. The fury felt by Selma's black community brought more adults to the demonstrations. The protest spread to the surrounding counties.

In nearby Marion, where Coretta and Martin were married, there was a church rally on the night of February 18. Four hundred black people started a protest march toward the courthouse. Alabama's public service director, Colonel Al Lingo, was on hand with state troopers. The troopers, joined by white toughs, advanced upon the marchers. They began to beat up any black person in sight, swinging night sticks and smashing heads. Jimmie Lee Jackson, twenty-five years old, tried to protect his mother. A trooper shot him in the stomach; he was taken to a hospital.

The bloody Marion march exposed the cruelty of the police. Jimmie Lee Jackson died. Three thousand angry blacks went to the memorial services, one in Selma, another in Marion. Martin King sensed that the popular mood had reached a peak of fury. It was time to call the people back into the streets with a fresh, dramatic demonstration. He announced that there would be a march to Montgomery to take a petition for the vote directly to Governor George Wallace. It was scheduled for Sunday, March 7.

There was bitter opposition to this from SNCC. SNCC leaders were critical of King. They did all the hard, dangerous work of voter education, they said, of training local people to assume the leadership in voting campaigns. Then King moved in, took direction of the local movement, and got the glory. They decided that SNCC would not support the Montgomery march as an organization, but its individual members could make their own decisions as to whether they would participate or not.

Opposition came, too, from Governor George Wallace. He issued a statement forbidding any march along U.S. Highway 80 leading from Selma to Montgomery. Rumors spread that if King insisted on marching the troopers would shoot to kill. Coming as they did after Marion, these rumors were not to be taken lightly.

Martin King was under heavy pressure. The campaign was coming to its climax; he neither wished to be jailed at this time for defying the governor nor to antagonize Lyndon Johnson, who also did not want the demonstration to take place. King canceled the march and left for Atlanta to preach at the Sunday Lenten services. SNCC leaders in Selma refused to back down. The march must go on, they said, whether Martin King was there to lead it or not. King, on the phone from Atlanta, finally agreed, but under one condition: The marchers must not go beyond the city line. If they did they would be outside the jurisdiction of the moderate Baker and at the mercy of Lingo and the state troopers.

Sunday afternoon, March 7, 1965, a line of men, women, and children began marching from Brown Chapel. Baker met them with orders to return to the church. They did, but later a larger group of over six hundred started out. Hosea Williams and John Lewis led the way. Shey and Rachel were there, scared but determined to "put on their marching shoes" as King often teased them. Two abreast, the line moved through Selma's back streets toward the downtown section, then turned southward.

The mood was one of happy fellowship. The sky was clear, the air calm and mild. Along the roadways early spring flowers, jonquils and forsythias, heralded a season of change. As the people marched, their voices filled the air with freedom songs. Many of them carried bedrolls, knapsacks, and containers of food. They might have been on a church picnic. Scores of newsmen walked with them.

It was peaceful, too. Sheriff Clark had left town, gone to Washington to appear on a television program, "Issues and Answers." Al Lingo had driven to the airport to meet him. What the marchers could not know was that the two officers had hurried from the airport and would be arriving at a bridge from one side, just as they approached from the opposite direction.

The Edmund Pettus Bridge arched across the Alabama River and overlooked downtown Selma. The steel structure measured three-tenths of a mile and provided a gateway from the city to U.S. Highway 80, leading to Montgomery. As Sheyann described, "You have to walk up it like it's a little hill. We couldn't see the other side, we couldn't see the troopers."

Williams and Lewis, veterans of confrontations, never missed a stride when they did see them. The crowd followed.

"Oh, my Lord!" A woman cried in horror at the sight.

About one hundred state troopers clad in blue jackets and blue helmets held clubs and had gas-mask pouches slung over their shoulders. An additional one hundred possemen were on horseback, like cavalry ready to charge. Photographers watched from the sidelines. As though on cue in a staged drama, a car came at full speed, bringing Sheriff Clark, still wearing his business suit but holding a tear-gas canister.

Major John Cloud, who led the troopers, stepped forward. "You are ordered to disperse and go back to your church or to your home," he said.

"May we have a word with the major?" Williams asked.

"There is no word to be had," Cloud answered. "You have two minutes to turn around and go back to your church."

Lewis recalled the next move. ". . . Everybody, every single person just sorta kneeled, over the Alabama River. . . . Over half the people were still on the bridge, had not made it across."

"Troopers forward!" Major Cloud suddenly ordered.

Television cameras whirred, recording the sequence of shocking scenes that made viewers recoil in horror when they saw them. Possemen rode horses into the crowd of defenseless marchers as though charging an invading army. Handbags and knapsacks scattered everywhere. Amid the screams of those hurt, possemen moved about, swinging nightsticks. Then a gray cloud began to spread, "Gas" someone moaned. The wretching and choking began. Even as they tried to run, the horsemen pursued the people, beating them at every step.

Cries from the victims told the horror: "Oh, God, they're killing us!"

"Get those God damn niggers!" cheered onlookers from the sidelines.

Amelia Boynton later said, "The horses . . . were more humane than the troopers; they stepped over fallen victims."

Sheyann Webb saw horsemen running toward her wearing those awful masks. She remembered, "Some of them had clubs, others had ropes or whips, which they swung about them like they were driving cattle."

The victims escaped to Brown Chapel, with possemen chasing them to the church steps. The strong risked their lives to save the injured. Men linked arms and formed stretchers to carry the helpless. Others picked up frightened children. Through her tears Sheyann saw the horses bearing down upon her. "So I kind of knelt down and held my hands and arms up over my head. . . ." At that moment Hosea Williams grabbed her under his arms without missing a stride.

In Brown Chapel parsonage doctors and nurses who had come to join the march administered first aid. Many people required hospital treatment.

Later that night Selma's blacks came together, seeking comfort from three sources that for centuries had strengthened them in times of oppression: their church, their prayers, and their songs. Sheyann remembered how the singing reflected the changing emotions. "It was like a funeral sound, a dirge. . . ." "*Ain't Gonna Let Nobody Turn Me Round.* . . ." the people began to pick it up . . . "Ain't gonna let no horses . . . ain't gonna let no tear gas—ain't gonna let nobody turn me 'round. Nobody!" Singers felt the strength flow from one person to another. Shey recalled, "Just all of a sudden something happened that night and we knew in that church that—Lord Almighty—we had really won, after all. We had won!"

Events at Edmund Pettus Bridge threw the nation into turmoil. People set out both for Washington, D.C., to press for civil rights legislation, and for Selma, to offer support. Thousands participated in sympathy marches all over the country.

Martin King was caught between the demands of his own supporters, who wanted to march again no matter what happened, and the insistence of Lyndon Johnson that there must be absolutely no second confrontation. King chose to heed Washington rather than endanger the passage of the civil rights legislation, which was his goal. On March 9 he led a token march from Brown Chapel to Pettus Bridge, then turned the procession around and marched it back again.

Movement people in Selma were disgusted by this anticlimax. But the national crisis was rekindled with the murder in the Selma streets of Reverend James Reeb, a white minister from Boston who came to Selma to take part in the March 9 demonstration. When they heard this news hundreds more people converged upon Selma. The demand was raised more insistently than ever: There must be a new federal law to guarantee and to protect the right of citizens to register and vote.

On Monday, March 15, President Johnson delivered a speech to a joint session of Congress asking for the passage of a voting rights bill. "It is wrong—deadly wrong—to deny any of our fellow Americans the right to vote," he said. Black Americans, he went on, "have awakened the conscience of this nation. Their demonstrations have been designed to call attention to injustice, designed to provoke change, designed to stir reform. They have called upon us to make good the promise of America. . . . Their cause must be our cause, too. . . . It's all of us who must overcome the crippling legacy of bigotry and injustice."

Justice Department lawyers set to work to draft a bill to be submitted to Congress. The literacy tests, which had for so long barred black people from the right to vote, were declared illegal. Where state officials continued wilfully to deny people the right to speedy registration, the federal government was authorized to appoint federal registrars to register the voters instead.

The time for a second march to Montgomery had now come, this time not to demand a civil rights law, but to support its speedy passage. The federal court gave permission for the march; the president stated that he would tolerate no state interference with this peaceful demonstration. On Sunday, March 21, over thirty thousand marchers set off from Brown Chapel.

Martin King was happy. He talked and joked with black people who lined the roadside to watch the procession pass. When a crippled old man realized that this friendly person who had shaken his hand was *the* Dr. King, he could only say "Oh Lordy!" and then, "I just want to walk one mile with y'all." Poor downtrodden people gained an unsurpassed sense of dignity from a smile, a word, a handclasp from Martin King.

There was a mood of delirious happiness, too, among the marchers. After about 7 miles the group separated. An advance group tramped the narrow country roads for the whole 50-mile trip to Montgomery; the rest returned to Selma. Three days later these Freedom Walkers arrived on the outskirts of Montgomery. There, all the other marchers joined them for the grand entrance into the city. On Thursday, March 25, twenty-five thousand Americans marched together for the last three miles.

At the head of the ranks were Martin King and Coretta, Ralph Abernathy and Juanita, Ralph Bunche, John Lewis, Bayard Rustin, Roy Wilkins, A. Philip Randolph. Daddy King was there, as were Coretta's mother and father and Martin King's sister, Christine, and his brother, A. D.

Going through the Montgomery streets the marchers passed Dexter Avenue Baptist Church and assembled around the Alabama state capitol, where the Confederate flag flew from the high dome. Governor Wallace refused to accept the people's petition demanding voting rights and an end to police brutality. Instead, he stood at the window of his office and peered down at the scene below.

There were the usual speeches; the marchers waited for Martin King. Ralph Abernathy introduced him: He stood up where Jefferson Davis had taken the oath as president of the slaveholding Confederacy. "We're on the move now," he said. "March on until racism is annihilated. . . . March on the ballot boxes . . . on segregated schools . . . segregated housing. . . . Let us march on to the realization of the American dream."

The familiar, well-loved cadence built to a climax. Telling his supporters that they were still in for a season of suffering, he asked rhetorically how long it would take before they were free? "Not long," he answered, "because the arm of the universe is long, but it bends toward justice. How long? Not long, because mine eyes have seen the glory of the coming of the Lord. . . ."

What began as the Montgomery Movement had come full cycle. Rosa Parks occupied a seat of honor on the platform. She symbolized the beginning, when only a few black people began to walk, led by an unknown young preacher. Ten years later all America, even the world itself, was being touched by the freedom revolution that had grown from that beginning.

☆ ☆ ☆

On August 6 the Voting Rights Act of 1965 became the law of the land. It would, in the following twenty years, reshape the political and social life of the South.

EPILOGUE: THE WILDERNESS
AND THE MOUNTAINTOP, 1966-68

> *Nel mestro del cammin di nostra vita*
> *Mi ritrovai per una selva selvaggia*
> *Che la diritta via era smarrita*
>
> (In the middle of man's allotted
> life span I found myself in a
> wilderness where no path was to
> be seen)
>
> Dante Alighieri

In 1965 Martin King was thirty-six years old. He had led many campaigns waged in order to win, for black people, full citizenship. Martin King's nonviolent approach had won great victories; they were recorded in the federal statute book as the Civil Rights Act of 1964 and the Voting Rights Act of 1965. It would be many years before the full meaning of these acts, in terms of freedom from discrimination and gains in black voting power, would become apparent. These acts were important steps forward on the road to freedom. They were won at the cost of titanic sacrifice. A generation of young people had given all its energies to the struggle. Living at a pitch which could not be sustained indefinitely, many were exhausted; they had burned out.

The changing mood of these young people was embittered by disillusion with Martin King's philosophy of nonviolence. It was one thing to practice nonviolence in the solidarity of a big demonstration, when the TV cameras were trained upon you, when the violence practiced by the segregationists upon the innocent could be recorded for all the world to see. It was quite another thing when, as an organizer traveling the lonely roads of Mississippi, for example, you confronted your murderer without a witness to record your death. Acceptance of nonviolence, in this context, obliged the victim to renounce that very right he was claiming for the black people: the right to be protected by the U.S. government itself.

By 1964 many SNCC workers in the Deep South viewed segregationists not as sinners to be prayed for but as deadly enemies.

The civil rights movement had been, from the start, interracial. After the March on Washington it began to disintegrate, to split up along racial lines. The split was both a symptom of the movement's crisis and a cause of its destruction.

This situation became apparent in the reaction of the black community in the North to civil rights successes won in the South. Neither the Civil Rights Act of 1964 nor the Voting Rights Act of 1965, important as they were, had very much to offer the black people of the North, who were the overwhelming majority of black people in the United States. Nobody in the North contested the right of black people to register and to vote. Nor were there laws barring them from equal access to schools, hotels, restaurants, buses, and trains.

Black Northerners faced different problems. Dire poverty penned Northern blacks in rat-infested ghettoes in the inner cities. There they were exploited by white landlords and white storekeepers and brutalized by racist white police. They were the first victims of street crime generated by poverty and despair. The root cause of this problem was crass discrimination both by white employers and white trade unionists who barred black people from job training and from access to skilled jobs. What had this civil rights revolution really won, Northern blacks asked themselves, when it had won the right to drink coffee in a restaurant or to vote? Big deal! Northern blacks could drink coffee where they pleased, and they possessed the vote. Small good it had done them.

During the middle sixties the Northern inner-city ghettoes began to go up in smoke as black slum dwellers made bonfires in Watts, Chicago, Newark, Detroit, and a dozen more American cities. These riots were put down, frequently with the loss of black lives, by white police and white troops. But they called attention to intolerable conditions of life that human beings were no longer willing to accept. They raised the issue of the need of a second revolution to bring to oppressed people the social and economic rights without which they could no longer survive.

At the same time the attention of Americans was being turned away from social reform at home to war abroad. U.S. military involvement in Vietnam escalated rapidly with the coming of Lyndon Johnson to the presidency in 1965, and the sending of thousands of American soldiers directly into combat.

This involvement was a tragedy for all Americans, but above all for the black people. It meant that the beginning of a second phase of the freedom revolution, for the winning of social justice, would be indefinitely postponed. It is one of the iron laws of our history that you may have social reform or war, but not both at the same time. Black youth now would win skills, jobs, and pay not to rebuild American cities but to kill other people in far off-lands.

Martin King was deeply troubled by the Southeast Asian adventure, which he regarded as a war against an Asian people in which the country ought never to have become involved. In 1967 he began to speak out publicly against this war and the government that was conducting it.

These antiwar speeches provided J. Edgar Hoover with an excuse to hound him. The director of the FBI had already amassed a voluminous file dealing with King's personal life. King knew that whenever he reserved a hotel room it had usually been bugged by the time that he moved in. FBI agents might even be installed in a neighboring room, equipped with earphones and tape recorders.

Amidst the confusion, violence, and bloodshed of the middle sixties the movement for freedom had come to a halt. Martin King found himself in the wilderness. Nonetheless he

Rev. Martin Luther King, Jr. photographed with (right to left) Ralph Abernathy, Jesse Jackson, and Hosea Williams on the balcony of the Lorraine Motel in Memphis, Tennessee on April 3, 1968. On the following day an assassin's bullet felled him at this very spot. (AP/Wide World)

set about planning for the second phase of the civil rights revolution: the struggle for social justice. He announced a "Poor People's March" in Washington, D.C. to dramatize the condition of the poor. It was scheduled to take place in the summer of 1968.

In March of that year King received an appeal from the sanitation workers of Memphis, Tennessee, who were mostly black, to help them in their strike for a living wage. It was a plea from very poor workers that he could not ignore. He flew to Memphis.

On the evening of April 3, 1968 he addressed the workers at a public meeting in the Masonic Temple. He was thirty-nine years of age, weary, and uncertain about what he ought to do. The old movement was over; a new one had not yet been born.

What if he had died, he asked his audience, when he was stabbed in 1958 in Harlem? He would have missed the greatest experience of his life in the freedom struggle of the black

On April 9, 1968, grieving people in tens of thousands followed Martin Luther King, Jr. for the last time as his body, in an open cart drawn by mules, passed through the streets of Atlanta. (AP/Wide World)

people. There were difficult days ahead, he said, days of confusion and doubt to live through. He was not discouraged by
this, on the contrary. "It really doesn't matter with me now.
Because I've been to the mountaintop. . . . I've looked over
and I've seen the Promised Land." Then he gave the people
whom he had served so well his final promise, and his
prophesy. "I may not get there with you," he said, "but I want
you to know tonight, that we as a people will get to the
Promised Land. So I'm happy tonight. I'm not worried about
anything. I'm not fearing any man."

It was the conclusion of a mature activist. Revolutions become successful not by one but a score of titanic efforts. Those
who start the struggle seldom live to witness its completion.
This is not surprising. They fight not for themselves but for
humanity.

The movement for freedom will go on, King said. The tide
will rise again.

☆ ☆ ☆

On April 4, 1968, Martin Luther King, Jr. was killed by an
assassin's bullet while standing on the balcony of the Lorraine
Motel, Memphis.

SIGNIFICANT EVENTS IN THE LIFE OF DR. MARTIN LUTHER KING, JR. AND THE CIVIL RIGHTS MOVEMENT, 1954–1968

1929   Martin Luther King, Jr. is born in Atlanta, Georgia January 15

1944   King enters Morehouse College at age fifteen

1948   King is ordained a Baptist Minister

1951   King graduates from Crozer and begins studies at Boston University toward a doctorate

1953   Martin King and Coretta Scott are married in Marion, Alabama

1954   The U.S. Supreme Court declares public school segregation unconstitutional

       Dexter Avenue Baptist Church installs King as pastor

1955   Boston University awards King his doctorate in systematic theology

Rosa Parks is arrested for violating Montgomery's bus segregation ordinance on December 1

The Montgomery Bus Boycott begins on December 5

1956   U.S. District and Supreme Courts rule that segregation on city bus lines is unconstitutional

Montgomery city buses are integrated on December 21

1957   The Southern Christian Leadership Conference (SCLC) is founded in Atlanta

Dr. King speaks at the Prayer Pilgrimage in Washington and is acclaimed a national leader

The courage of nine black students who integrate Central High in Little Rock, Arkansas focuses attention on school desegregation

1958   Dr. King is stabbed while autographing his new book, *Stride Toward Freedom: The Montgomery Story*

An interracial Youth March dramatizes support for school integration

1959   Coretta and Martin King tour India and study Gandhi's life and nonviolent direct action techniques

Dr. King resigns as Dexter's pastor to devote his time to civil rights projects

1960   Student sit-ins bring a wave of protest across the South

The Student Nonviolent Coordinating Committee (SNCC) is founded

The 1960 Civil Rights Act becomes law on May 6

Dr. King is arrested during a sit-in in Atlanta and kept in prison; intervention by John Kennedy gives the senator support from black voters, which helps to elect him president

1961 The first Freedom Riders leave Washington by bus on May 4

A second group of Freedom Riders leaves for Jackson, Mississippi and is imprisoned, but refuses to accept bail

1962 Many SNCC Freedom Riders stay in the South to help local leaders develop civil rights projects

Dr. King helps to lead the Albany Movement

1963 SCLC launches the Birmingham Movement and Dr. King is jailed while leading a march on Good Friday

"Letter from Birmingham Jail" is written

The "Children's Crusade" creates the crisis needed to focus national attention on lack of justice for blacks in the South

The March on Washington marks the largest civil rights demonstration in history; Dr. King delivers his "I Have a Dream" speech

1964 The St. Augustine campaign brings the issue of states' rights into the open

"Mississippi Freedom Summer" led by student volunteers spotlights lack of justice and opportunities in Deep South states

The Nobel Peace Prize is awarded to Dr. King on December 10

The 1964 Civil Rights Act outlaws segregation in public accommodations

1965   The Selma Campaign begins a massive drive for voting rights

"Bloody Sunday" at Edmund Pettus Bridge causes Americans of all races to join the Freedom Movement

Dr. King leads the Selma to Montgomery march, and speaks to twenty-five thousand in front of the Alabama state capitol

The 1965 Voting Rights Act is signed by President Johnson

1966   Dr. King begins a movement in Chicago to call national attention to conditions in city ghettos

1967   Dr. King speaks out against America's involvement in the Vietnam War

Dr. King announces a Poor People's March to call attention to jobs and freedom for the poor, black and white

1968   Dr. King goes to Memphis on April 3 in the hope of leading a peaceful march in support of striking sanitation workers

Dr. King is fatally shot on the balcony of a Memphis motel

Dr. King is buried in Atlanta on April 9

The Martin Luther King, Jr., Memorial Center, later renamed The Martin Luther King, Jr., Center for Social Change, is established by Coretta Scott King, the King family, and other associates. It houses valuable research materials on Dr. King's life

1986   A bronze sculpture of Dr. King is unveiled in the U.S. Capitol.

January 15, Dr. King's birthday is officially celebrated as a national holiday, marking the first official national holiday in the United States to honor a black American

FOR FURTHER READING

MARTIN LUTHER KING, JR.

Dr. King's own writings shed much light upon his life, his personality, and his struggles. *Stride Toward Freedom: The Montgomery Story* (New York: Harper and Row, 1958) is a good place to start. His other books are: *Why We Can't Wait* and *Where Do We Go from Here: Chaos or Community?* (New York: Harper and Row, 1964 and 1967, respectively). *Strength to Love* (Cleveland, Ohio: World Publishing Co., 1963) is a collection of Dr. King's sermons expounding the message of the Gospel and the meaning of nonviolence.

Valuable and interesting works by family members are Coretta Scott King's *My Life with Martin Luther King, Jr.* (New York: Holt, Rinehart and Winston, 1968) and Martin Luther King, Sr.'s *Daddy King: An Autobiography* (New York: William Morrow, 1980).

A number of biographies of Martin Luther King, Jr. have been published. Recommended are: Lerone Bennett, Jr., *What Manner of Man: A Biography of Martin Luther King, Jr. 1929-68* (Chicago: Johnson Publishing Co., 1967); Laurence D.

Reddick, *Crusader Without Violence* (New York: Harper and Row, 1959), the first full-length biography written by a friend and history professor who took part in the Montgomery bus boycott; and David L. Lewis, *King, A Biography* (Urbana: University of Illinois, 1978. 2nd ed.), a fact-filled work good for reference. William Witherspoon's *Martin Luther King, Jr.: To the Mountaintop* (New York: Doubleday, 1965) is a tribute enriched by two hundred photographs.

THE FREEDOM MOVEMENT

There are many accounts of the freedom struggle of the 1950s and 1960s provided by people who took part and who were witnesses to history in the making. In *My Soul Is Rested: Movement Days in the Deep South Remembered* (New York: Putnam and Sons, 1977) Howell Raines brings together interviews with key participants and with whites who opposed them. Daisy Bates' *The Long Shadow of Little Rock* (New York: David McKay, 1962) is the story of the nine black students who integrated Central High, told by the Arkansas NAACP leader who risked her life to counsel and lead them. Elizabeth Huckaby's *The Crisis at Central High: Little Rock 1957-58* (Baton Rouge: Louisiana University Press, 1980) provides the inside story of the school itself, the struggle and growth that took place there among the students during the first year of the integration process. In *Freedom Ride* (New York: Simon and Schuster, 1962) Richard Peck, one of the leaders, relates the epic of the first Freedom Ride. Juan Williams' *Eyes on the Prize, America's Civil Rights Years, 1954-1965* (New York: Viking Press, 1987) recaptures the history of this period as seen by the participants and serves as a companion volume to the TV series of the same name.

Sally Belfrage's *Freedom Summer* (New York: Viking Press, 1965) is a personal account of the dangers involved in the Mississippi Summer Project as well as the wonders of the experience. Elizabeth Sutherland brings together in *Letters from Mississippi* (New York: McGraw Hill, 1965) a collection of writings by student volunteers. In *Selma, Lord, Selma*

(University: University of Alabama Press, 1980) Frank Sikora documents the recollections of Sheyann Webb and Rachel West Nelson in a vivid and moving account of their involvement both with the voting rights struggle and with Dr. King.

The above may be supplemented by Harvard Sitkoff, *The Struggle for Black Equality 1954-80* (New York: Hill and Wang, 1981), which provides a useful overall view of the movement and of Martin King's relationship to it. Guy and Candace Carawan's *We Shall Overcome! Songs of the Freedom Movement* (New York: Oak Publications, 1965) gives the words and music of many freedom songs that tell of the courage, endurance, and vision of the young people who sang them.

ARCHIVAL MATERIAL

Taylor Branch's narrative biographical history, *Parting the Waters: America in the King Years, 1954-1963* (New York: Simon and Schuster, 1963), and David J. Garrow's *Bearing the Cross: Martin Luther King, Jr. and the Southern Christian Leadership Conference* (New York: William Morrow, 1968) provide exhaustive guides to archival sources. The major depositories for King's personal and organizational papers are the Martin Luther King, Jr., Center for Nonviolent Social Change, Atlanta, Georgia, which houses thousands of items pertaining to Dr. King, including speeches, correspondence, and interviews, and the Martin Luther King, Jr. Collection, Mugar Library, Boston University, Massachusetts. This collection houses at least 83,000 items relating to King's life up to about 1964.

The Ralph J. Bunche Oral History Collection, Morland-Spingarn Research Center, Howard University, Washington, D.C. is a valuable resource for recorded interviews with Rosa Parks, John Lewis, and many other key movement leaders.

INDEX

A